To

My dear

Carol

I KNOW HIS TOUCH

I KNOW HIS TOUCH

Luba Bershadsky
with Ada Millington

CROSSWAY BOOKS ● WESTCHESTER, ILLINOIS
A DIVISION OF GOOD NEWS PUBLISHERS

Cover illustration by Dwight Walles
First printing, 1984
Published in the United States of America
Library of Congress Catalog Card Number 83–72042
ISBN 0–89107–299–3

CONTENTS

1 REVERIES

Next to me Nina Andreyeva snored. Spasms from her nightmares disfigured her face. In all the prison nights I had lain squeezed on the wooden plank between Nina Andreyeva and Lena Zhilinskaya a smile had never mirrored Nina's night thoughts.

At least Nina and Lena were fortunate to sleep, I thought. My own increasing insomnia the last few months had begun to bar even this final escape from the torments of Kengir Prison Camp.

That night, to make matters worse, I longed to turn over, a consideration too minor to trouble me most nights. But Nina and Lena lay beside me, seemingly asleep, and I could not bring myself to disturb their short hours in another world.

I settled for pulling the two dirt-encrusted blankets, spread over the three of us, slightly closer to my chin and tried to content myself with modest comforts. But even that small movement had dislodged the blankets from my blistered feet wrapped in two black cotton rags which barely resembled stockings.

I wiggled my toes to create warmth in my frozen feet—my once-beautiful ballerina feet. In all the twelve years I had danced in the Bolshoi Theatre, I had not neglected even one night to wear warm woolen stockings to bed and to rub rosewater on my feet in the morning. "You can recognize a lady by her hands and a ballerina by her feet," Mother always said.

Perhaps it was the pleasant memories of my mother which finally helped me fall asleep that night. But a bloodcurdling scream from somewhere across the barracks jarred me awake.

"The lights! They are turning them off! They're going to kill us!" I heard the frenzied voice but at first could not find the face in the rows of women lined along the wall on my side of the barracks. Then I saw her—a fear-streaked face, its furrows washed by tears. I also spied the glint of jagged glass in the woman's hand. "I'll cut my wrists before I let them kill me," she bleated.

"Masha, the glass. Give me the glass. Be sensible." A second woman crouched beside the first, her voice soothing. "It's only a bad storm outside. That's what made the bulb flicker. But it's lit now. They're not coming."

In an instant I understood Masha's nightmare. Every Soviet prisoner knew the legend. Day and night the dangling, unshaded electric lights in our barracks burned. How else could the hunters watch their prey? It was only when the hunters readied themselves for the kill, prison legend said, that the lights went out.

Mercifully, after Masha's scare I managed to sleep again until my usual waking hour of five o'clock—a full thirty minutes before most of the barracks would rise. At first I had despaired at losing those treasured minutes of sleep, but in the last months I had begun a new morning ritual.

It had begun with the rattling window next to our bed, which had initially seemed only another source of torture. All night shafts of Siberian cold shot through the spaces around the loose window panes, stabbing and stinging. The only equitable way to contend with this fierce enemy, Nina, Lena, and I had agreed, was to rotate turns sleeping beside the window. One morning, during my turn sleeping next to the window, I had awakened at five, inching as far from the hated cold as possible, my mind full of memories of another Siberian prison when I had awakened one icy morning to find my hair frozen to the iron bed. I could still feel the pain when I wrenched my hair free.

Now I lay still, feeling both glad and guilty that in one more week I would be able to switch places with Lena and be at least a foot further from the window. Suddenly, I chanced to notice the way the light bulb on the rafter above us illuminated the ice embroidered on the window. There, etched in delicate white detail, was a whole world. And because I wanted to discover it so desperately, I had soon discerned a map of my beloved Moscow on the window.

I explored my map. The strong, straight line toward the center—that would be Strastnoi Boulevard fronting Pushkin Square. Twenty-two years ago on a spring day in 1932 my older brother,

Styopa, had escorted me, a sixteen-year-old, past Pushkin Square to the gilded doors of the Bolshoi Theatre for the first time. Thousands of times after, I had entered that fairytale world.

My memories took me back to August 1932 and the day Rostislav Vladimirovich Zakharov, my ballet mentor from childhood, who was then the chief choreographer at the Bolshoi, had summoned me to his office.

"I have decided, Luba, that you should dance Odile in my production of *Swan Lake*," Zakharov announced. "I know you are young, but after considering all the Bolshoi ballerinas, I have decided you are the best dancer for this part and I am placing my highest hopes in you. If you fulfill my instructions exactly you will be a dazzling Odile."

From the age of four when I had begun dancing, my life in ballet had been a parade of successes. But accustomed as I was to this succession of triumphs, Zakharov's announcement left me stunned. How could I, a sixteen-year-old and newcomer to the Bolshoi, dance the second leading role in Tchaikovsky's *Swan Lake?* But in seconds my strong resolution had submerged any reservations, and I was thanking Rostislav Vladimirovich and accepting his offer. I not only could dance Odile—I would become Odile, the love-stuck magician's daughter consumed with unrequited passion for Prince Sigfried.

As frenzied as Odile in pursuit of her prince, I flung myself into rehearsals for my new role, my only disappointment the discovery that the famous prima ballerina Marina Semyonova who was dancing the lead part of Odette would not be rehearsing with the rest of our troupe until the dress rehearsal.

Semyonova, acclaimed across Russia, had for several years been my idol and meeting her my dream as a child dancer in Kiev. I was not surprised, therefore, that so exalted a person as Semyonova should not mix with the rest of us dancers, but I was disappointed. Would my meeting with this woman who had mesmerized me for years occur only when we finally danced together on the same stage?

On January 27, 1933, deep into the rehearsals for *Swan Lake*, I arrived one morning at the Bolshoi. As usual a crowd of people lined the performers' entrance, straining for a glimpse of the ballet stars. I, not yet a star, glided through the crowd unrecognized. This morning the crowd clustered exceptionally thick and clamorous and

I heard someone say, "Please, Marina Semyonova . . . your auto-graph." I whirled toward the voice, but could not immediately see Semyonova's face, only her elegant figure attired in a dark green coat with mink collar and matching mink hat.

Struggling to see Semyonova, I studied the faces of the crowd, as adoring and transfixed as I by the famous ballerina. Finally Semyonova moved toward the door. I leaped to hold it open for her. She smiled as she entered and said, "Thank you, Lubasha. How kind of you."

Lubasha! "But how do you know me?" I stammered. Semyonova, laughing gaily, circled my shoulders with her arm. "It is a secret, a big secret," she replied with the same rippling laughter. "But I will tell you.

"For several weeks I have been coming to my rehearsal an hour early. I go to an unlit loge on the right side of the stage and watch you rehearse. Zakharov has often spoken of you, and I have waited with great impatience to meet you. Of course your gift is from God, Lubasha. Besides your talent, your proportions are magnificent. A famous career awaits you, and you will be loved by the public. And it is for that we give ourselves," Semyonova concluded, kissing me before we parted.

Of all the compliments showered on me during my ballet career, none had been so shimmering and significant as Marina Semyonova's. After twelve years of dancing, I for the first time felt myself fully a ballerina.

For two years I danced *Swan Lake* and just as Zakharov and Semyonova had predicted, the role of Odile brought me fame all across the Soviet Union.

My major part as Odile was in the second act by the lake. As the curtain opens on act two, Odile, attired in a pink dress, stands at the front of the corps de ballet—twenty men and women—all in white. It is Odile who leads the other dancers to center stage, in a languid adagio which discloses her hopeless desire for Prince Sigfried.

At the close of this scene all the dancers leave and Odile stands alone on the stage. This was my moment and I savored it. The stage, the thousands of prestigious people in the audience, and even the two hundred piece orchestra directed by the famous Meliick Pashaev were at that moment, like the theatre floodlights, all focused on me. I whirled into leaps and fouettes executed so swiftly I did not feel my own body but only Odile's frenzied passion. Spent from this display, my Odile, at the end of the second act, sinks into slumber by the lake and awakens to discover Odette, Sigfried's true love, among the swans who appear in the morning.

After my last dance in the fourth act, I always stood in the stage wings, waiting for the curtain calls. And, as predictable and thunderous as Moscow summer storms, applause engulfed us. I stood next to Semyonova, luxuriating in the acclaim, smothered with flowers and well-wishers.

After the final curtain call, we dancers would always surround Semyonova and escort her to her dressing room, usually to an accompaniment of tears of happiness and awe. Zakharov, who knew we wept from joy, sometimes joked, "If this continues I shall have to rename this ballet, Lake of Tears!"

A half hour had passed and the barracks had started to stir, but I was with Marina Semyonova at the Bolshoi and had not noticed. Now, at 5:30, I could not escape the gong, thundering through my reveries, reverberating my window world, forcing me back into the stench and squalor of my Siberian prison.

"*Vstantye!* Get up!" A guard swung wide the barracks door to rasp his command into our room even before the gong had subsided.

When I was a child, my mother or my nanny, Dunya, always woke me. Both woke me in the same manner, stroking my forehead with their hands. But with my eyes closed, still wrapped in the warmth of sleep, I always knew whose hand it was—Momma's, soft, smooth, and fragrant with French Coty perfume; or Dunya's, leathery, large, and scented with lemons freshly sliced for our morning tea.

Both Momma and Dunya wove a web of security and comfort around my childhood—a cocoon I took for granted. And they never disagreed. Therefore, one day Dunya surprised me when she confided, "You know, I am a little bit afraid of your mother, Lubasha."

"Afraid of Momma?" I echoed, wondering how anyone could fear my *mamochka*.

"You know how I love you, Lubasha," Dunya said, helping me into the white linen nightgown which she washed and ironed every day. "Maybe someday I won't please your mother and she won't want to keep me."

That night I watched my mother while she prayed before the

candlelit icon in a corner of her bedroom. When she had ended her prayers, I repeated Dunya's remark. Momma kissed me, made the sign of the cross over me, and offered no comment about my conversation with Dunya.

The next morning I entered my mother's bedroom. There sat Momma in her stately rose satin armchair, braiding the flaxen hair of Dunya bowed on a footstool at my mother's feet.

Gentility seemed to cloak my mother as comfortably as the elegant seal fur cape she always wore to the theatre. The daughter of a Polish aristocrat, Franz Kentrszhinsky, my mother was born in the picturesque Ukrainian province of Sosnovka on the shore of the Dnieper River in a grand four-story beige brick mansion, which after the Bolshevik Revolution would be converted to a tuberculosis sanatorium.

A forest of birches and pines unfolded behind the Kentrszhinsky house, and in front an oval pond bordered an apple orchard. Every morning Katya, the lady's maid, ran to the pond, tinkled a silver bell, and a school of goldfish swam to the shore for a breakfast of yesterday's butter-roll crumbs.

Except for the father, Franz, the Kentrszhinsky family was all women—Ekaterina Alexeyevna, the mother, and nine daughters. Kentrszhinsky, who had hoped for a son, protectively devoted himself to his daughters, permitting them to leave his house only escorted by a governess.

With so many daughters, governesses, and servants, the Kentrszhinsky household bulged, swelled often by picnics, parties, and balls. Battalions of young men in black tuxedos and white gloves came to court the lovely Kentrszhinsky daughters, who often stayed awake all night after the guests had gone to discuss the merits of every waltz partner.

Franz Kentrszhinsky considered piety even more important for his daughters than parties, and on Sundays, with Franz at the head, family and servants filed from the house, filling six carriages and three pews at St. Nicholas's, the blue-domed Russian Orthodox Church that rose from the golden Ukrainian fields of Sosnovka.

At home Franz himself always led family prayers, his daughters circled around him, logs flaming in the massive granite fireplace. The prayers lasted longest in winter, my mother always said, when the sisters delayed climbing into their cold beds.

For years, a succession of weddings provided the main social events of the Kentrszhinsky family. The three older sisters all married wealthy young men. The fourth sister, Stasia, my mother, married Leonti Grigorievich Bershadsky, the only son of an impoverished noble family who lived in a modest home near the Kentrszhinsky estate.

Leonti's father, a schoolteacher, tutored his only son, known to the neighbors as "the studious one." By the time he had become a teen-ager, Leonti had begun to notice Stasia, the slender Kentrszhinsky daughter with luminous gray eyes.

Stasia had been aware of Leonti long before, although the only times she saw him were when he walked in a park in town where Stasia often came with her German governess, Edna.

One day, sitting beside Stasia on a bench in the park, Edna noticed the words, "Leonti, Leon, Lyonya," written on Anastasia's sketching tablet. The governess confided Stasia's attachment to the girl's parents, who approved of the serious young student and arranged the marriage.

"But if you marry my daughter, you must manage the factory that Stasia will receive as her dowry," the elder Kentrszhinsky stipulated. This was how in 1872 at twenty-two years of age, Leonti became the director of a nail-manufacturing plant employing eleven thousand people.

I was Stasia and Leonti's sixth child, christened Luobov, a name chosen by my father, which means love. By the time I was born in 1916, my father had turned the nail factory over to a Kentrszhinsky brother-in-law and moved to Kiev with his family in order to seek treatment for stomach cancer.

My father's illness cast a pallor on my family's prosperous life in the spacious new apartment on Kiev's Mikhailovskaya Street. But both my father and mother strove to preserve stability in the family despite Father's grave illness, which Kiev doctors diagnosed as terminal.

As always, on Christmas 1916 a fir tree towered in the center of our parlor. Dunya sprinkled salt at the base of the tree for snow and, around the tree, my father arranged twelve sturdy papier-mache, red-capped Father Frosts, each with a bag slung over his back with the name of a month. December was the smallest figure and January the largest, almost as tall as my oldest brother, Styopa.

By the fall of 1916 when Styopa was already a teen-ager, I was only taking my first steps on the veranda of our Kiev apartment. Dunya brought a large basket of plums from the garden. I stood up from my blue velvet pillow, tottered toward the basket, and fell. Dunya scooped me up and exclaimed in Ukrainian, "The child's walking!"

Poppa embraced me and remarked wistfully, "Will I live to see my Lubochka running?"

2 BEGINNINGS

Father, ill as he was, had not secluded himself from the turmoil his beloved Russia was experiencing the last year of his life.

Above all, Father worried about the war and specifically about Styopa, now twenty years old and ripe for the army. Would Styopa, like millions of other young Russian men, die somewhere in Europe in the senseless struggle with Germany that seemed to promise so little reward to Russia?

And, as if the war were not enough agony for one country, there was the violent political and social tumult wracking Russia internally, threatening to rip away the fabric of czarist society with its watchwords of autocracy, orthodoxy, and nationalism which my parents had known all their lives.

It was not that my father was opposed to change. "I am a proponent of gradual democratization," he would tell Grandfather Kentrszhinsky, who shuddered at the prospect of any alterations in his aristocratic world.

"The Duma, that's our best hope," Father would argue with Grandfather Kentrszhinsky, unaware that the Duma, Russia's first truly representative governing body, would survive only a few months longer than he.

Father died in February, two months before my second birthday. One month later Czar Nicholas II abdicated, relinquishing three hundred years of Romanov rule.

Styopa, more than any other member of our family, had been influenced by my father's sympathy for reform. But because he was restless and impetuous, Styopa could not settle for less than a role in the new Bolshevik Revolution.

"I'm glad Leonti didn't live to suffer this sorrow," Grandfather Kentrszhinsky groaned when he learned Styopa had joined the Bolshevik army. With my grandmother too ill to discuss such subjects, Grandfather Kentrszhinsky remonstrated about Styopa's Bolshevism with my mother, who comprehended only a little of the political significance of events swirling around her.

Although as repelled as my grandfather by the crude manners of the Bolsheviks, my mother felt compelled to defend her son. "Father, you know Styopa. Ever since you gave him a pony when he was ten he has always wanted to be in the cavalry. He is young and adventuresome. To him it is above all an opportunity for fame and fortune," Mother surmised, analyzing—as the future revealed—Styopa's revolutionary motives better than Styopa himself understood.

But Styopa's recklessness was regarded as idealism by his superiors, and he rose rapidly in the rag-tag Bolshevik army. It was in 1918 when Styopa was only twenty years old and a commander in the first cavalry of Semyen Michailovich Budyonni that my brother most distinguished himself.

During February, the worst month of the winter of 1918, Budyonni, his assistant (General Clementi Efrimovinch Voroshilov), and Styopa were stranded in a blizzard on a military train twenty kilometers from the nearest station. In the thick of the storm, Voroshilov collapsed with a heart attack. Styopa hoisted the general on his back and carried him twenty kilometers to the nearest doctor, saving Voroshilov's life.

In 1918, with both my father and Styopa gone, my mother, Dunya, and we five children who were still at home moved to a smaller apartment on Kiev's Bolshaya Zitomiskya Street, close to the shops and St. Sofia Russian Orthodox Church.

In the new apartment my mother always kept the shades in the parlor pulled. Sometimes in the evenings she sat in a black tulle dress at the ebony piano in the parlor and played and sang:

> *Fate leaves its mark—a bell tolls faintly,*
> *Again I see your face so clear,*
> *The breath of former days blows freshly,*
> *Your note before me yet lies near . . .*

Grandfather Kentrszhinsky, still spry at ninety-eight, came at least several times a year all the way from Sosnovka to visit my mother. He nestled me against his cologned gray beard while he spoke with my mother. "I'm worried about you, Stasia dear." The conversation would almost always begin while Dunya placed glasses of tea in filigree holders before my mother. Ceremoniously my mother would pour steaming tea from a burnished brass samovar into the glasses, nodding as my grandfather spoke.

Balancing me on one knee and resting his glass of tea on the other, I could sense Grandfather's solemnity when he lowered his voice and said, "The Bolsheviks—they are barbarians, Stasia. You know they have confiscated our nail factory. They're not going to stop until they have destroyed the old world and all of us who are a part of it. That includes you, my dear!"

"I have the jewels from you and Leonti. There is enough for me to care for the children. God will provide," my mother would reply, permitting me a sugar cube, but not a grown-up glass of tea.

"But you are only forty-one. You are still young, Stasia. Why don't you remarry? I can arrange it all," Grandfather would offer, a flicker of the power of the old days returning to his eyes.

"I can't imagine being the wife of another man. For me there is only Leonti," Momma would demur, folding her linen napkin beside the samovar.

"And what of Lubasha?" Grandfather would pat my head as he plucked me, my mother's baby, like a feather to furbish his argument.

"I will rear Lubasha to be a lady, of course."

But Grandfather Kentrszhinsky, even at ninety-eight years, was a man accustomed to managing his family. Despite my mother's disinterest, he encouraged prospective suitors to call, whom my mother, with adamantine grace, refused to receive.

When I was four years old, Grandfather Kentrszhinsky died and no more suitors came to call on my mother. "He couldn't reconcile . . . he couldn't reconcile"—I sometimes overheard my mother speak to Dunya about Grandfather after his death. It was only as an adult that I realized she had been referring both to the Bolshevik Revolution and her refusal to remarry.

Before he died, Grandfather had urged my mother to change

her dark dresses for brighter colors, an alteration my mother with her stern sense of decorum did not think proper until two of my older sisters were married in the same year—both in matches largely arranged by my mother. My sister Ira and her studious engineer, Valya, moved to Moscow where Styopa, also married by this time, had already settled. My sister Dusya and her husband Jan stayed in Kiev.

Only two years after my sisters' marriages, a double tragedy struck my family, returning my poor mother to mourning with two heavy strokes. Within six months of each other, my sister Vera, seventeen, died from blood poisoning and my brother Seryozha, twenty, died from a rheumatic heart.

Now my mother never played the piano, which stood draped with a black cloth in the parlor. In evening conversations around the fireplace I often overheard Momma speak to Dunya about the sad succession of events in the Bershadsky family. "*Ad astra per aspera* . . . through difficulties to the stars," my mother would sigh.

"God gives and God takes away." Dunya would always offer the same sagacious reply.

God to me was most closely associated with the right-hand corner of my mother's bedroom where she knelt every evening before a blue wall covered with icons illuminated by glowing candles. My mother's bowed head, folded hands, and reposed prayer created a picture that reminded me of the icons themselves.

On Sundays I always went with my mother to "God's House," as she invariably referred to the Orthodox church near our home. A little like Momma's icon corner, the larger, luminous world under St. Sofia's blue-and-gold-spangled domes was in comparison a universe.

Momma kept three candles burning in her icon corner in the evenings, but under St. Sofia's domes banks of candles in rows like a congregation flickered and flared, casting shadows on the gilded icons which seemed as alive to me as the worshipers kneeling before them. The candles wafted thick waxen smoke that mingled with the incense from the priest's censer and came curling back toward the worshipers.

My mother always knelt longest before an icon of Mary, the mother of Jesus. Mary's dress was as dark and her eyes as sad as my mother's. "Don't speak louder than a whisper to the Holy Mother," my mother would instruct, helping me to kneel.

"Where is the baby Jesus? Why didn't you bring him with you?" I whispered to Mary.

But then I tired of the conversation. I watched my mother's lips moving, her stillness broken only by the sign of the cross she made swiftly at her breast. Why did she speak so long? I squirmed, and when my mother seemed so absorbed in her prayer that I was convinced she must have forgotten me I edged away from her to observe a *babushka* near us light a candle. I stepped closer to watch the way the *babushka's* hand trembled as she transferred the flame.

On the way home from St. Sofia my mother and I usually stopped at a French bakery, its small room redolent with the aroma of raisin-filled *bulochki* baked that morning. Usually my mother allowed me to select pastry—one box for our family and one for an impoverished family whom we would visit that afternoon.

But that Sunday Momma marched straight past the bakery. "You were naughty in church, Lubasha . . . squirming and fidgeting," my mother accused in the special low voice she used when she spoke to me of something important.

My mother scolded me so seldom that I felt humiliated. I hung my head and swiftly contrived an excuse that I thought would please her: "I was looking for God."

But my mother was not convinced. "When you go to church, God is already there, looking at you from all sides."

Besides such impromptu instruction in theology, my mother devoted herself, as she had assured Grandfather Kentrzhinsky she would, to rearing me as a lady. Lessons in English and German and readings by my mother from Tolstoy, Shchedrin, Turgenev, and Pushkin began long before I started school.

Occasionally my mother set her lessons in my playroom. Preoccupied with changing the hats of my ten china dolls, I would hear a knock on my door. When I opened the door my mother, wearing her hat and gloves and coat, stood before me. I would greet my "guest" and escort her into my room, and we would repeat the game until I could play the perfect hostess. Sometimes I asked to play cooking or washing dishes—like Dunya. "No, that is not for you, Lubasha," my mother would say.

I discovered how ladies ought to behave one day when I laughed at a disheveled boy with a dirty face. My mother's voice was as modulated as always, but the displeasure it conveyed hurt more than a spanking. "I am ashamed of you, Lubasha. Ladies do not laugh at others' misfortunes. Ladies help the poor and the weak. I thought my Lubasha was a lady."

One spring morning when I was four, I was jumping rope with some neighbor children in our apartment courtyard, swaying with a cadence I had learned while watching the maids dance at Grandfather Kentrszhinsky's *dacha*. I could see my mother above me watching from the window alcove of our apartment, her arm resting on a pink satin pillow. As I was jumping, a young woman entered the courtyard and stood observing us children for several minutes. Her gaze rested on me.

"What is your name?" she asked when I had stepped away from the rope.

"Lubasha."

"You jump very beautifully. Who taught you?"

Before I could answer, the lady was smiling and saying, "Would you like to be a ballerina?"

I did not understand the word "ballerina," but I did like the lady and the prospect of what sounded like a new game. I nodded my head.

"Please take me to your mother," the woman said.

That woman with whom one chance meeting changed my life forever was Zina Ieronimovna Yasinskaya, a ballet teacher and choreographer who had once been a student of Isadora Duncan. Recently Zina Ieronimovna had moved from Kharkov to Kiev, where she decided to open a ballet school.

That spring I became one of Zina Ieronimovna's first four students, meeting for three lessons a week. Within a year Zina Ieronimovna's school had grown to forty students. The successful school soon attracted the attention of local Soviet authorities, who demanded that the school, like all organizations in the new Communist system, be placed under the jurisdiction of the government. The authorities also assigned the studio a name—Iskra or Sparks, after Lenin's famous journal which had ignited the Bolshevik Revolution.

I was entranced by the ballet uniforms and costumes at Zina Ieronimovna's Iskra studio. Even for classes we wore red tunics, wide red ribbons in our hair, and white slippers—colors, I suppose, suitable to the studio's revolutionary name. For performances, Zina Ieronimovna kept a whole closet—even more fascinating than my mother's—filled with fluffy tutus and a kaleidoscope of character costumes.

I adored Zina Ieronimovna, who transformed our strenuous lessons and eventually painstaking performances into what seemed to me a perpetual game. Even my mother, with her unbounded faith in my abilities, marveled at how swiftly I learned under Zina Ieronimovna's tutelage.

Zina Ieronimovna, young and beautiful, managed to treat us as both pupils and peers, often dancing with us. When we performed pieces from *Dance macabre* by Saint-Saens, Zina Ieronimovna, exquisite in a long white silk dress, danced the part of the dying woman. Two boys portrayed death and the rest of us children represented corpses.

By the time Zina Ieronimovna's studio had expanded to forty students, Iskra dancers were presenting performances at many theatres in Kiev and even occasionally traveling to other nearby cities and towns in the Ukraine.

I was four when I danced my first solo in *Rosinki (Dewdrops)*. I pirouetted in my white tutu across the stage, gracefully shaking imaginary dewdrops from my hands. In *Rigoletto* I became a butterfly. Suspended by pulleys over the stage, four of us Iskra students in bright yellow and red butterfly costumes hovered in the air through the scene when Rigoletto wanders through the forest searching for Gilda.

In another dance, my friend Katya was a cat and I a mouse. The most difficult moment was when the mouse, not knowing the cat is stealthily creeping up behind, sits scratching its nose. I begged my mother to catch a mouse so I could observe how it scratches its nose. "We don't have mice in our apartment," my mother said.

In one dance, all forty of us children were snowflakes. Zina Ieronimovna, to my delight, appointed me to execute a solo somersault from the bottom of a pyramid of snowflakes. When my moment came, the pyramid did not shift back far enough and my backbend landed me in the lap of a violinist in the orchestra pit below. The audience laughed and clapped and, far from feeling embarrassed, I felt I had accomplished a particularly clever feat.

Drop by drop during those early years of my career, a steady stream of approval and adulation was swelling. When I accompanied my mother to church or ballet classes, passersby sometimes stopped to talk with my mother and exclaim, "It's the darling little girl from Iskra. How proud you must be of her!" They would pat me on the head and call me their "Little dewdrop," "little mouse," or just Lubochka.

Even the director of the elementary school across the street recognized me, I discovered one fateful day. For months I had watched throngs of schoolchildren enter the school's gates each morning, and I had yearned to join them. One morning, while my mother was in another room, I took Tolstoy's *Resurrection*, the book my mother had been reading, stepped out the door, and crossed the street.

"We have a new one!" the children chanted when I edged into a classroom. The teacher took me to the school director who smiled and said, "Ah, it's the little girl from Iskra." Nevertheless the director clasped me firmly by the hand and escorted me back across the street to my mother.

My mother received me coldly and decreed my punishment. For three days I would not be able to leave the house—even for ballet class. I did not dream of arguing with my mother, but thinking I might alleviate my punishment, I did permit myself to inquire meekly, "Did the Holy Mother punish Jesus?"

It was the year I turned seven that my busy, blissful ballet world nearly collapsed. That year I had finally entered the school across the street, speeding through my homework to rush to my ballet lessons with Zina Ieronimovna, which had now increased to four times a week. One afternoon when I arrived with the other students for class, a stranger met us to tell us that classes had been canceled indefinitely. Zina Ieronimovna had been taken to the hospital with meningitis. Two days later our teacher, only thirty-three years old, was dead.

About three months after Zina Ieronimovna's death, a notice appeared in the Kiev newspaper. Rostislav Vladimirovich Zakharov, the ballet master of the Kiev Opera, the notice said, was inviting all students from Iskra Studio to try out for places in his studio.

From Zina Ieronimovna's students, who now numbered about one hundred, Zakharov chose ten. I was among the ten to whom

Zakharov's announcement of acceptance was coupled with a stern lecture on the demands of classical ballet. "You can expect my studio to be much stricter than Zina Ieronimovna's," Zakharov stated in a blunt manner that seemed to match his flinty eyebrows and bald head, which also made him appear much older than his twenty-four years.

A dancer who had not been able to make a career of ballet because of his short height, Zakharov was as demanding as he had warned.

"Good afternoon, Rostislav Vladimirovich." Always accompanied by my mother, I would greet my new teacher and bow to him in the same mannerly way Zina Ieronimovna had instructed us. Then, with my mother's assistance, I dressed—another aspect of ballet about which Zakharov enforced strict dictums. Our uniforms, white silk working dresses with a single skirt, should always be clean and pressed. Our hair must be pulled back tight from our faces and pinned neatly on the tops of our heads so that Zakharov could observe clearly how we positioned our necks and heads.

During our limbering-up exercises, Zakharov stood silently observing us. When the lesson began, we took our positions at the bar, spaced precisely one extended leg's length from each other. Zakharov stationed himself in the center of the classroom with a rubber baton which he used to tap our legs into proper position.

First we went through the various positions at the bar; then there was the center work away from the bar; then different combinations and various leaps. "Don't turn your body with your feet," Zakharov would call to us. "You cannot be called a ballerina until you no longer feel your legs," Zakharov would chant, his exhortations interspersed with position calls.

We learned five basic positions for the legs and eight for the hands and an endless succession of variations in between. But the basic positions were always in the same progression, which Zakharov said a true ballerina knew to be inviolable.

One morning a hapless classmate who arrived late for a lesson was nearly expelled. "Don't you know the sequence can never be broken?" Zakharov shouted.

And thus day after day Zakharov drilled ballet's exacting disciplines into us, perfecting its basic positions which are to ballet what an alphabet is to a writer.

In addition to my lessons and performances at Zakharov's studio, my teachers at school often organized amateur plays and programs, always assigning "Luba ballerina," as the other children called me, leading roles.

But there was one role at school my mother would not permit me to play. The new Bolshevik state, Soviet parents were repeatedly informed, expected all children to belong to the Communist youth organization—the Young Pioneers. But my mother kept postponing my membership. "We will wait," was all she would promise when I would beg to join.

Nearly all the children at School Number Nine were wearing the large red neck scarfs which were the symbol of the Young Pioneers and attending its meetings from which I was excluded. I—who had never felt censure in my life—began to feel an outsider.

One morning I was summoned to the school director's office. Besides the director, another man, whom I recognized as the tall mustached adult leader of the Young Pioneers at School Number Nine, was present. He beckoned me to a chair and said kindly, "You know, Luba, it is very important to be a Young Pioneer. It is what our Grandfather Lenin wants for all Soviet children."

Once when I had come home talking about "Grandfather Lenin," my mother had said curtly, "Lenin is not your grandfather." Although I was not at all certain who Lenin was, I now nodded my head obligingly.

"What work did your father do before he died?" the Young Pioneer leader asked, steering our conversation in another direction.

"He owned a nail factory. But it was contifiscated," I replied, stumbling over the word confiscated which I had heard Grandfather Kentrszhinsky use.

The school director and Young Pioneer leader both snickered at what I thought must be my incorrect pronunciation. But then the school director said, "And I thought you were a Soviet girl, Luba. But you are a bourgeoise, I see. We will be talking to your mother."

That night I recounted my conversation with the two men to my mother and the next morning discovered that she intended to accompany me to school. When I asked why Mother was wearing her velvet hat and fur cape, usually reserved for Sundays and concerts, she replied haughtily, "To show the difference between us and them, Lubasha. We are 'former' people. We are not like them."

"My daughter is not joining the Young Pioneers. You know yourself that the children carry on like hooligans, breaking into churches during services and mocking believers. At school it is your business to educate my daughter in academic subjects. It is my business to rear her and form her character. Please do not ever speak to her again about the Young Pioneers." I don't recollect all that my mother said, but I do recall the way the director meekly nodded his assent. Occasionally in later years in prison I would recall this conversation, which, from the perspective of prison, seemed nearly miraculous. Had there really been a time when a functionary of the Soviet state agreed that some entity besides the state ought to be permitted some control over a Soviet citizen?

For almost a year nothing more was said about my membership in the Young Pioneers. But then the subject arose through what promised to be yet another triumph in my career.

Clementi Efremovinch Voroshilov—the same Voroshilov whom Styopa had so heroically rescued during the Revolutionary War and who was now the chief commander of the Red Army of the Soviet Union—was visiting Kiev, and all the elementary schools were organizing a reception to greeet him. Galina Fyodorovna, the music teacher, chose me to give a greeting to Voroshilov on behalf of School Number Nine. I stood in the first row, holding a large bouquet of red carnations to present to Voroshilov, when suddenly the Young Pioneer leader was scowling down upon me.

"Where is your red scarf?" he snapped, apparently not remembering the nail factory or my mother. "You are a Pioneer, aren't you?"

"Yes," I lied in a frightened, small voice.

"She's lying, she's lying, she's not a Pioneer," the other children chimed, perhaps gratified to see Luba ballerina for once humiliated.

The Young Pioneer leader snatched the flowers from my hands and bestowed them on a gangly girl next to me who was wearing a red scarf. "But I don't know the greeting," the girl stammered.

"That's not important," the Young Pioneer leader glared. "What is important is that Comrade Voroshilov receive the flowers from the hand of a Young Pioneer."

That night I ran home crying to my mother. Although she stroked my hair when I buried my head in her lap, she concentrated more on the lie I had told than on the indignity I had suffered. "You will probably encounter such experiences many times in life," my mother said with a prescience which would have broken her heart if she had known how prophetic her words were. "You should not have lied. We cannot please everybody. It is God we must please. Always consult your conscience, and if it is pure that means that God is with you."

Although my difficulties in school had brought a few stabbing shafts of darkness into my light-flooded world, there were no shadows on my hours at Zakharov's studio. Zakharov, it was true, was strict and his lessons arduous, but I reveled in the challenge of ballet and in the compliments that I had now come to expect to fall like snowflakes every time we performed outside the studio.

Inside the studio, Zakharov was parsimonious with compliments, purposely prodding me to greater achievements by erecting new challenges before me like mountain peaks which I could never quite scale. A masterful motivator who perceived my strong sense of competition and thirst for success, Zakharov gave me only enough commendation to keep me striving.

Zakharov's rare approval, when it did come, took a form that at first mystified my mother. The first time Zakharov tweaked my nose with his fingers was when I, only eight, achieved sixteen foutees without a pause. Zakharov's nose-pulling, I knew, expressed approbation as surely as all the admiring adults who patted my head after performances. And it was Zakharov's approval that mattered most.

"Why did Rostislav Vladimirovich pull your nose today during the lesson?" my mother asked the first time she observed this ritual. "Did you misbehave?"

Despite my mischievous temperament, I was already at eight years old too dedicated to ballet to be tempted to any misdemeanors in Zakharov's studio. There was too much at stake . . . too many laurels to be won. The year I was eight the closest reward was pointed toe shoes, the kind Tamara Veraksa and all the other real ballerinas in the Kiev theatre wore.

When I was nearly nine, Zakharov permitted me to begin wearing toe shoes. I trembled with excitement the day that Zakharov and a committee of three doctors checked my legs and feet to determine if they were strong enough for the shoes. Zakharov had warned us all that we risked breaking a leg if we wore pointed shoes before our muscles were adequately developed. I think I might have taken the risk had the choice been mine, so exalted did it seem to acquire what I considered "real ballerina shoes."

Zakharov's greatest compliment came to me when I was nine. That year our whole class knew that the Kiev Opera Theatre's ballet company was preparing to perform Tchaikovsky's *Swan Lake*, choreographed and directed by Zakharov who would also dance the part of Sigfried.

Zakharov announced that he had decided to incorporate one of us children as a black swan dancing a two-minute solo in the third scene. "I will watch and choose the best black swan," Zakharov promised.

To dance with the adult ballet company was a glamorous, dizzying prospect. Besides dancing my best for Zakharov at lessons during the day, I began borrowing my mother's black feather fan, unfurling it while I caracoled in Arabesque poses before my mother's mirror.

One weekday when my mother escorted me home from ballet, we stopped on our way at the French bakery for petit fours, a purchase I understood must signal an extraordinary event. "I'm expecting a guest. Rostislav Vladimirovich Zakharov will come to tea today," my mother announced nonchalantly.

"Zakharov!" I squealed, hoping desperately that my teacher's visit might be related to the black swan role. But to my dismay I discovered my curiosity must be postponed.

"My talk with Zakharov must take place without you, Lubasha," my mother announced, dispatching me to the courtyard.

From the same courtyard where I had once met Zina Ieronimovna, I now spied Zakharov, flowers in hand, alighting from a horse-drawn taxi. He entered the gate and with his free hand hoisted me in the air. "*Molodets*, Lubasha—good girl," he said. Such a shower of affection I surmised could only be for the black swan.

Now, besides school and regular ballet lessons at Zakharov's studio, there were the rehearsals for *Swan Lake* and performances. The practice with my mother's fan had not been wasted. For the real performance, I wore a black tutu and tights and two huge black feathers on my head.

When the first notes of Tchaikovsky's music sounded in an adagio in the second act, I came *pas de barre* onto the stage, my head hanging down, my hands crossed on my chest, and felt myself fully a swan. Unlike Tchaikovsky's Odette, I did not wish to be transformed back to a girl.

The stream of acclaim I had experienced before now swelled to an ocean. As I was the only child in the ballet company, the other dancers mothered me. Balletomanes doted on me, smothering me after every performance with candy, fruits, kisses, and compliments.

Often my mother, who attended every performance, would stand by, shaking her head and saying, "Don't make her too proud." And at home she repeated her admonitions against pride. "If ten people like you, it doesn't mean the whole world likes you. The audience may clap for you now, but you will be forgotten and they will be cheering for somebody else in the future."

Zakharov too made a point of pulling me back to reality. "Technical perfection isn't enough, Lubasha. That is essential, but it is only a foundation. I want you to feel your part . . . to become your part so completely that the audience does not even think of you, but loses itself in the role you are portraying."

When *Swan Lake* finished after three years and eighty performances, Zakharov chose me and three other students from his studio to perform regularly with the Kiev Ballet Company. With all facets of my life sparkling, I glissaded into my teen-age years.

Now in addition to the adults who showered me with candy and flowers, a new group of admirers began to appear backstage at my door after ballet performances—young men laden with gifts and amorous expressions, which both flattered and frightened me. One evening after a performance, a young man with earnest eyes and shy smile stood clutching a bouquet of pink and white carnations, waiting for me backstage. He stammered some compliments about my dancing and introduced himself as Nikolai Borisovich Razumov, the grandson of Boris Petrovich Razumov, the famous Kiev sculptor.

"I would like to write a poem about you, Luba Leontievna," he blurted, blushing.

Nonplussed, I swiftly thanked him for his flowers, whispered "No, good-bye," and shut the door in his face.

By the time I was nearly fifteen, I did have a boyfriend, Volodia Bogdiukevich, a medical student and the son of my father's friend, the engineer Pytor Bogdiukevich. Since my father's death, my mother had become close friends with Volodia's mother, an educated, cultured woman, and Volodia and his parents often came to call on my mother. On such occasions Volodia's father always wore his elegant engineer's hat, a black beret trimmed with gold buttons.

Occasionally my mother permitted Volodia Bogdiukevich to escort me to my ballet rehearsals. But always when we left the studio we would meet our mothers who "happened" to be strolling in the area.

Several weeks before my fifteenth birthday, my mother bought me brown suede high-heel shoes. "You are an adult now," Volodia teased. To celebrate my fifteenth birthday, my mother planned the first party she hosted in our home since my father's death.

"We will invite your friends from the ballet studio and Volodia and his parents," Mother declared.

Dunya cooked and prepared for weeks for the party. There was red wine for the men, pink champagne for the women, and strawberry punch for my friends and me. Black caviar, pickled cucumbers, marinated watermelon and apple slices stood in silver trays at both ends of the table. Dunya had ringed the center dish, European woodland grouse, with a condiment of cranberries, a delicacy for which she had dickered with tradesmen for two months to procure enough for my party.

When the other guests had gone, Volodia's parents and my mother sat visiting on the balcony, leaving Volodia and me alone in the sitting room by the piano. I touched the tall wicker basket of white lilacs beside us, Volodia's birthday gift to me. "They are lovely, Volodia. But how did you ever find white lilacs in April?"

"Love made me keep looking," Volodia laughed, but suddenly he was pulling me toward him, kissing me. "Lubasha, I love you. When I finish the institute, we can marry. Do you want to be my wife?"

After the Bogdiukeviches left, I joined my mother at her evening prayers before the icon corner in her bedroom. When her prayers concluded I announced, "Volodia kissed me tonight by the piano, *Mamochka.*"

My mother was silent for what seemed to me several minutes before she said, "Take care this is not repeated, Lubochka."

"I promised Volodia I would marry him," I hurried on, thinking this admission would justify the kiss in my mother's eyes.

Mother sighed and stared at the icon of Mary, but spoke to me. "You and Volodia are talking about this altogether too soon, Lubasha. Marrying is not a simple matter, and I hope that when the time comes for you to marry, you will allow me to participate in the choice of your husband. You are still a child. As I have always told you, God is with you, Lubasha. If you want to be happy, allow him to lead you and choose a husband for you. Don't hurry life. It is already too short."

My mother did not refer to this subject again, and my dates with Volodia continued as before. But something had changed between Volodia and me. Now when we parted he kissed me on the forehead. But it was the other kiss by the lilacs which hung in my memory.

One night as we were parting, Volodia pretended to pout and instead of his customary kiss on my forehead, he turned away from me. "When a girl loves a boy, she kisses him first," he asserted, searching my face for response.

"That is impossible," I said, wishing I dared kiss Volodia but imitating the imperious tone my mother used in resolving matters of right and wrong.

It was two months before I turned sixteen that an announcement from Zakharov shattered my world like thunder on a cloudless day. That morning at Zakharov's studio had begun with the usual exercises at the bar, but before we moved on the floor Zakharov spoke. "You will all be transferred to another teacher. I have been invited to Moscow to become a choreographer at the Bolshoi Theatre and I am accepting."

A few days after this thunderbolt, Zakharov visited my home. This time, as had been the case seven years earlier, his visit augured well for me. Now I was in the room when Zakharov said to my mother, "I have been Luba's teacher since she was seven, and I don't want to lose her. Will you permit her to come to Moscow and continue her studies with me at the Bolshoi?"

"Of course, Rostislav Vladimirovich," my mother said. "It is a very great honor."

As devoted as I was to ballet, my first thoughts centered on home. "But I will be so lonesome for you and Dunya and Volodia," I wept when Zakharov had gone, slurring and softening my pronunciation of Volodia's name lest my mother should suspect he had supplanted or even occupied an equal place in my affections.

"Of course I will miss you too, Lubasha." My mother smoothed my hair as she had done when I was a child. "But as soon as we are able, Dunya and I will move to Moscow. It is a great honor to be chosen by Zakharov to come to the Bolshoi and you will be with Styopa and Ira," my mother reminded. In all the excitement, I had nearly forgotten my brother and sister in Moscow.

On a spring morning in May I said good-bye to my mother, Dunya, and Volodia at the train station. Volodia, with my mother beside us, kissed my forehead and placed an enormous white pencil in my hand with the words, "To my dear Lubochka," etched on the side. Dunya had removed her white starched kerchief to wipe her tears. Mother was thrusting a straw basket with food for the trip into my hands. She kissed me, embraced me, and made the sign of the cross over me as I stepped onto the train.

As the train pulled away I spied Volodia on the platform. I lifted his pencil and kissed it. The last sight I saw was my mother in her blue dress with a white collar and white hat embracing and consoling Dunya.

3 BOLSHOI

Perhaps it was the rhythm of the train rushing toward mysterious Moscow that filled me with a feeling of destiny and distracted from the Kiev farewells. My mother's face in her small white hat still filled my mind, but speculations about my new life began to creep in at the corners of my thoughts as the train wound through Ukrainian villages with sagging wooden huts and bands of sturdy women planting a checkerboard of spring gardens.

Three steps onto the platform in Moscow, I found myself wrapped in the embrace of a beautiful woman with blonde hair whom I had never met before. "It's our Lubasha," Maria, Styopa's wife exclaimed, recognizing me from a photo my mother had sent. Then Styopa, grown bald in the ten years since he had moved to Moscow, was engulfing me in a smothering hug.

Although my sister Ira and her husband Valya also lived in Moscow, my mother had arranged by letter that I should live with Styopa and Maria, who possessed the larger apartment. After the Revolution, Styopa's career had advanced to the prestigious position of commandant of Moscow, and by Moscow standards Maria and Styopa's life was lavish. Besides a three-room apartment on the famous Gorky Street, they could afford a cook, and Styopa, the military mayor of Moscow, had a chauffered limousine at his disposal.

Zakharov had arranged for me to meet him at the Bolshoi the Wednesday after I arrived in Moscow. Styopa, commandant of Moscow though he was, seemed awed at the prospect of delivering me to the Bolshoi. "Shouldn't you wear gloves? Is that the dress Mother suggested you wear?" he worried.

Promptly at ten, Styopa escorted me to the Bolshoi's side service door. A dour woman in a gray uniform asked to see our passports. She scanned a list on her table and nodded at me. "Zakharov's student," she said, and waved me through the door but raised her hand, a barrier to Styopa. "There's no authorization for you, comrade."

Inside the Bolshoi's marmoreal halls, I searched for Zakharov's office, stopping passersby for directions. I asked one young man striding by who halted, held out his hand, and said with a grin, which I was soon to discover was his most characteristic expression, "You must be Luba from Kiev!"

"But how did you know?"

"Rostislav Vladimirovich is expecting you and so am I," the young man with the contagious smile replied. "I am Sasha Kranikov, and whether you want me or not Rostislav Vladimirovich has appointed me as your dancing partner," he announced with such good humor that I found myself smiling back at this irrepressible young man who would in 1949 be arrested and exiled to a Siberian labor camp on charges of telling an anti-Soviet joke.

Filled with thoughts of a partner—a prospect which I felt would catapult me into the adult world of ballet—I entered Zakharov's office. But Zakharov, although he welcomed me affectionately, soon ballasted my daydreams with reality. "You have already lost too many training days, Lubasha," he observed. "I am assigning you to my training group, and tomorrow you begin a regular practice schedule."

Zakharov's classes at the Bolshoi followed the same rigorous routine that they had in Kiev and I swiftly settled into their pattern, content to again be under the tutelage of my beloved teacher.

But slowly, like melting snow seeping into spring soil, I began to perceive what a radical change had occurred in my sixteen-year-old life. Thanks to Zakharov, I had been uprooted from Kiev and transplanted in Moscow—in the great Bolshoi Theatre, the most magnificent ballet company in the Soviet Union, if not in the world. Without even asking I had arrived at the Bolshoi, an achievement most ballerinas could only dream about.

Zakharov, my mother had always instilled in me, was a great artist. Now at the Bolshoi everyone seemed to concur with my mother's opinion. "He's a genius you know . . . He's the most innovative choreographer in the Soviet Union . . . You are Zakharov's pupil?"

But Zakharov, prominent as he had become, did not forget his unknown pupil from Kiev. One day in June, about a month after I had arrived in Kiev, he summoned me to his office.

"Lubasha, I want you to take the soloist exam," he announced. "I believe you are ready for solo roles, but of course you must first pass the exam before I can assign you a part outside the corps de ballet."

"But, Rostislav Vladimirovich, how can I possibly take the exam so soon?" Even I, uninitiated as I was in the Bolshoi world, by now understood that most of my colleagues had waited—often as long as five years—to try out to be a soloist. And even then, most had not succeeded.

"I will arrange it," Zakharov replied in a tone that signaled the matter was already settled. "I will schedule the examination for August. The fact that you are the only student whom I invited from Kiev will stir considerable interest in you. But that will probably also inspire the examination committee to be more exacting," he said, adding his customary challenge.

Because Zakharov believed me qualified to become a Bolshoi soloist, I did not, in the two short months before the examination, experience any profound pangs of doubt myself. "Rostislav Vladimirovich says he has a choice solo role in mind for me when I finish my examinations," I wrote confidently to my mother in Kiev.

The exams, Zakharov had warned me, would not consist of a specific repertoire which I could memorize and rehearse, but entirely of improvisations. However, even this uncertainty did not shake my confidence and calm.

When I left Kiev, my mother had tucked a small icon of Christ wrapped in a linen cloth in the corner of my suitcase. On the August day of my examination, I knelt in my dressing room and prayed. I heard the click of my door opening, but I continued to pray.

"Let's wait. She's praying," I heard Zakharov whisper. When I had finished Zakharov entered, accompanied by an older man with a kindly face, whom I had not met before. Zakharov introduced me to Nikolai Dmitrievich Garnik, the president of the Bolshoi reception committee and member of the Soviet Ministry for Cultural Affairs.

We spoke about the exam, but after Zakharov left Garnik lingered behind. "My child, I personally admire the fact that you pray," he said, placing a fatherly hand on my shoulder. "But in the future try to do this behind a locked door. It would be better if no one sees you."

By now the fact had penetrated my sheltered world that the Bolsheviks were antireligious. But no one had opposed my mother for attending church in Kiev. My mother never hid the fact that she prayed daily in the icon corner of our home. "Why shouldn't I pray?" I said, unable to think of any other response to Nikolai Dmitrievich's admonition.

Garnik continued in the same quiet, reasonable voice, at risk to himself, I realized later. "The Bolshoi Theatre is a romantic, beautiful world—isolated from the Soviet world. But you must not forget that it is also a Soviet establishment, and that carries certain demands that cannot be circumvented," he said vaguely. "You will need to heed my advice for your career."

Before leaving my dressing room, Nikolai Dmitrievich opened the door to check if anyone was outside. He swiftly closed the door, made the sign of the cross over me, and said, "Christ be with you," before slipping off down the corridor.

Nikolai Dmitrievich Garnik, my kindly protector, was, I soon learned, considered at the Bolshoi to be one of the best instructors of classical ballet. He was also a member of the old intelligentsia. Most importantly, he was the father of my good-natured ballet partner Sasha, who had changed his last name because he "wanted to shine with his own glory."

On the August day of my examination I stood in the stage wings, poised for my entry, listening to Zakharov's introduction commending my achievements in Kiev. From offstage I studied the audience arrayed under the Bolshoi's glittering crystal chandeliers. Bolshoi staff and Moscow artists more accustomed to the place of performer than spectator had been invited especially for my examination.

Zakharov walked back to the wings, and suddenly the audience was mine. I pirouetted onto the stage and thought I could detect the loud applause of Styopa, who sat with my family in the third row. I dropped a deep curtsy and then hovered, waiting for the committee's first call. Clear and quick as arrows the committee's commands shot through a microphone.

In an instant I was expected to match the movement to the music, also extemporaneously, since I did not know which pieces the orchestra would choose. Between calls from the committee, I glanced at Zakharov, who stood offstage, encouraging me with a wink each time our eyes met.

After an hour of improvisations, the exam concluded. Again I was curtsying, the floodlights were blinding my face, and I was certain from the frenzied applause that I had succeeded. I curtsied again as an attendant brought two burgeoning baskets of flowers— one from my family, the other from Sasha. In my dressing room I found a bower of flowers and well-wishers. Zakharov presented me with a gold pendant and a book about the famous Anna Pavlova. Styopa, for the first time seeing me dance on stage, embraced me through tears. "You were wonderful, Lubachka, wonderful!"

But still my celebration had not quite concluded. Styopa guided me to the theatre buffet. Zakharov and Nikolai Dmitrievich Garnik stood at the entrance beckoning us inside. Guests from the exam audience welcomed me with applause. The adults drank champagne and regaled me with toasts: "To Zakharov's best pupil ... to a new Bolshoi star . . ."

It was shortly after I had passed my exam that a visiting French ballet company performed at the Bolshoi. Sasha and I sat in the audience with other Bolshoi dancers, eager to watch the French dancers rehearse. But before the rehearsal began, a French choreographer attired in black tights carried a black box decorated like a birthday cake with golden candles onto the stage. He turned to speak to one of the Russian stage managers whom Bolshoi stage workers called "The Cat." The Cat walked to the edge of the stage, scanned the auditorium, and asked in a purring voice that may have accounted for his nickname, "Is Luba Bershadskaya in the audience?"

I stood up, bewildered and a bit frightened. The Cat motioned me forward and I flew to the stage. Still without knowing why I had been summoned, I found myself being introduced to the French choreographer. Suddenly he was thrusting the black-and-gold box into my arms. "To congratulate you on your success in passing your exams," he said. I opened the box and inside found a half-circle electric space heater. "We French know that Moscow is cold and a ballerina must keep her feet warm," the choreographer announced with a bow and smile.

That afternoon, inside Zakharov's office, I asked, "But how did they know about me, Rostislav Vladimirovich? How did they know in France that I had passed my exam?"

Zakharov pulled a clipping from his desk, which, to my astonishment, pictured me in my white tutu, executing a jete. "The French publish a paper on cultural events, and they make a special point of staying informed about Russian ballet—particularly at the Bolshoi."

But on this remarkable day Zakharov had not finished unwrapping surprises. "The French company has invited you to be their guest for dinner this evening at the Metropole," he announced.

"The Metropole!" I exclaimed, the elegant box that had held the heater slipping from my hands. But as quickly as my joy surged, it began to ebb as I remembered that sometimes Styopa took me to restaurants during the day, but never in the evening. Once when he and Maria were dressing for an evening dinner at a restaurant, I had sat pouting in their parlor. Maria sensed my hurt and embraced me.

"At the Bolshoi I am treated like an adult," I sniffed through tears, "but Styopa thinks I am a child."

"You are not quite yet an adult, Lubasha," Maria said with a smile, showing me a letter from my mother addressed to her and Styopa. Underlined was the command, "Do not take Lubasha to restaurants in the evening."

"I can't go. My mother would not approve," I now explained to Zakharov, who, I knew, understood my mother's principled ways.

When I returned home for dinner, carrying my new heater, Styopa met me at the door. He greeted me with a kiss and announced, "You can go to the Metropole. Zakharov and I have talked, and he himself will be your date."

In 1932 Moscow ladies wore long dresses to evening engagements. But my mother, not wanting to encourage a lady's social life for a girl, had not packed any long dresses for me. I did, however, have a blue velvet dress trimmed with a white lace bow on the bodice, which I wore that night with blue shoes and blue violets in my hair.

A doorman ushered Zakharov and me into the Metropole, and the gilded ballroom and lavish buffet table before us seemed to me more a prop from the theatre than the real world. Cold turkey slices garnished with liver pate, pickled mushrooms, and mounds of black caviar filled the table which stretched under shimmering crystal chandeliers.

A young Frenchman, whom I had noticed on stage when the choreographer presented me my gift, asked me to dance, and I noticed that he, unlike any man I had met before, wore cologne.

We danced magically, fluttering around a fountain that stood in the center of the room, the prince and princess of the ball. We were so engrossed in our dance that we did not notice when the other dancers left the floor and became our spectators. A woman with blonde hair and a lavender chiffon dress clapped her hands and shouted "Bravo!" and the other guests began to applaud.

Years later, in nine months of solitary confinement at Lubianka Prison, I was to reflect on the party at the Metropole. Was it possible that such a fantasy night had truly been a chapter of my tragic life?

As soon as I had arrived at the Bolshoi, Zakharov had immediately organized a rigorous training schedule for me. Even before my exams, in addition to my group training sessions Zakharov had begun to coach Sasha and me together, assigning us a repertoire which included both character and classical dances. My first debut with Sasha was in a Spanish dance, "Schelkunchik." "Look how perfectly matched they are. She stands just to the tip of his earlobe"— admiring snatches of conversation wafted to me from the audience the first time Sasha and I danced together.

But even the glamour of dancing with Sasha was superseded by the ineffable honor of being chosen by Zakharov in August 1932 to dance the role of Odile in *Swan Lake*. "Zakharov has bestowed a very great honor upon you, Lubasha," my mother wrote from Kiev. "And of course I am confident you will not disappoint him."

Each morning I rehearsed from ten to one with Zakharov, memorizing and repeating movements from sketches drawn by my teacher. Every afternoon I practiced these same movements privately with a pianist hundreds of times until they were perfect.

One day as Sasha and I walked past the Bolshoi box office on our way to practice sessions, we overheard a crowd of people discussing a sign at the Bolshoi ticket window which listed my name with Semyonova as principal dancers in *Swan Lake*. "Who is Luba Bershadskaya?" people were asking. "I've never heard of her."

"It's the girl from Kiev who recently passed her examination," someone said.

"And she is already dancing the part of Odile?" someone else exclaimed. "She must be talented."

"She is talented, and she is Zakharov's creation," the first voice said.

It was true. I was Zakharov's creation, molded and shaped by him as a dancer from childhood. Now in *Swan Lake*, Zakharov was again chipping, chiseling, polishing me to create Odile and I was obsessed with a desire to please him.

Zakharov's first requirement, I knew, was that I live the role of the lonely, miserable, rejected Odile. This task was not simple for me whose life had been saturated with love and success, but I forced myself to concentrate on Odile's plight until gradually I could feel her fear and frenzy permeating my thought and movements.

The transition from Luba to Odile for which I was striving so hard seemed to me particularly successful one morning during a rehearsal with Zakharov. Certain I had danced exceptionally well, I ran toward Zakharov and playfully positioned my face close to his, waiting for my teacher to pull my nose, the ceremony which from my childhood had symbolized his ultimate approval.

"Not yet, Luba. Not yet," Zakharov said and immediately started to describe a new movement I must learn. Zakharov's slight rebuff stung me. Fearful I might never be able to please him, I immediately redoubled my efforts to win his approval.

"You're practicing too strenuously," Styopa's wife Maria fretted when I extended my herculean practice sessions at the theatre and constantly concentrated on my role when at home as well.

One day three weeks after the episode with Zakharov I was leaving the theatre following a class. I felt a hand on my shoulder and before I could turn to see to whom it belonged, someone was gently pulling my nose. "Rostislav Vladimirovich!" I exclaimed, collapsing on Zakharov's shoulder and weeping.

"Go ahead and cry a little, my first Odile." Zakharov stroked my head. "Even though you are not a big star yet, you are a little star already."

From this moment, I felt myself to have conquered the steepest part of my climb, and as my prowess became more pronounced my practice sessions became slightly less strenuous.

Swan Lake premiered on February 4, 1933 to rave reviews from the critics for both Semyonova and me. The only remotely critical comment about me appeared in *Moscow Art World News:* "Bershadskaya possesses breathtaking proportions and technical perfection," the reviewer wrote. "But she is still too young to have experienced the range of emotions needed to truly enliven Odile."

Even while rehearsing *Swan Lake* I had continued to rehearse other soloist roles with Sasha for concerts. Although Sasha and I never spoke about the subject, we both possessed a driving determination to please Zakharov. As we succeeded, Zakharov permitted us to expand our repertoire which grew in one year to include a Gypsy dance in *Sleeping Beauty*, a Spanish dance from the *Nutcracker*, and a pas de deux from *Red Sails*.

Always searching for new mountains to conquer professionally, Sasha and I began in May 1933 to give performances outside the Bolshoi. These performances were arranged by Sasha's father through the organization Moscow Concerts, which controlled all performances in Moscow by Bolshoi performers. At first Sasha's pride was grazed to have to resort to using his father's influence to book openings. He recovered swiftly when he realized the extra money and public acclaim to be earned through these concerts.

By autumn 1933, Sasha and I were dancing in concert halls across Moscow, dashing in one evening to several engagements, with several hundred more invitations than we could accept arriving each month. After rehearsals all day at the Bolshoi, our stamina might have flagged at night had it not been for Vitaly Mikhailovitch Louewn, a blind masseur from the Bolshoi Theatre who with his wife Sonya accompanied us to performances—Vitaly massaging us between performances and Sonya catching cabs and organizing our costumes.

At each performance Sasha and I attuned our repertoire to the audience, dancing classical pieces for intellectual audiences and polkas and Ukrainian folk dances at the factory halls. The component that did not change from one hall to the other was an avalanche of applause, an elixir enabling me to dance twelve-hour days.

As our names splashed in ads and magazines and theatre bills across Moscow, people stopped to notice Sasha and me on the street. In December 1933 Zakharov choreographed a dance for us in honor of the new year's tree. Sasha represented Father Frost and I was Snegurchka, the traditional Snow Maiden. From the first performance the dance was a wild success, and Sasha and I used to joke that we had performed it on every stage in Moscow. That winter, walking on the street I became accustomed to hearing people point and call me "Snegurchka."

By letter my mother had agreed that I could perform in concerts outside the Bolshoi with Sasha. But although Momma had come to trust Sasha through Styopa's letters, she had nevertheless stipulated, "Luba is always to be accompanied by a chaperone."

On nights we weren't performing, Sasha and I, always accompanied by Styopa or another chaperone, relaxed by attending the theatre and often saw favorite plays several times. We never missed a play at the main theatres—the Art Theatre, the Vachtangov, the Maly—and we knew the names of all the actors and actresses.

Each of the theatres possessed their own stylistic trademarks, and it was not a case of which I loved best—I adored them all. During those years, Maly was primarily performing Ostrovsky's drama. The Art Theatre, led by the renowned Stanislavsky, was perhaps my favorite with a company which included Olga Knipper, and also Tachalov, Moskvin, Shevchenko, Sosnin, Tarasova, Chmelev, Plotnikov, and many other stars.

Bundled in the otter fur coat which Styopa had given me, I dashed from rehearsals to concerts to theatres. "I wonder if all ballerinas have so much energy!" Maria often exclaimed observing my frenzied schedule. To me it was all as invigorating as a Moscow snowstorm, with pleasures flying at me so fast I hardly had time to savor one before another was appearing.

4 LOVE

"Well, Luba, whom do you love now that you are seventeen?" Maria teased me one day when she came upon me writing a letter to Volodia, with whom I had carried on an ardent correspondence since arriving in Moscow, although most of my ardor centered on descriptions of my new life in Moscow.

"Have you forgotten Volodia for Sasha?" Maria teased. I frowned. Of course I had not forgotten Volodia, nor my promise to marry him.

The conversation was forgotten, but a few days later Maria was unusually eager that I be home for dinner. "We are having guests. Two friends of ours whom we would like you to meet." That evening I was introduced to Andrei, twenty-five, and Zhan, twenty.

"Zhan," I laughed when he repeated his name. "Are you French? Why do you have such a non-Russian name?"

Zhan bowed and nodded coldly.

"I am sorry. I hope I didn't offend you," I swiftly said.

"That is all right. I am not offended," Zhan replied, but his tone belied his words. All through dinner he paid me little attention, a neglect I was not accustomed to encountering from young men and which only enhanced my interest in Zhan, who now seemed totally absorbed in conversation about juridical science.

"May I ask how you are so well informed about this subject?" I asked finally when it appeared that the handsome Zhan was not going to make an effort to converse with me.

But Andrei answered for Zhan. "Zhan is too modest to tell

you himself. He is a student—an excellent law student—and is finishing his studies this year."

"A lawyer with such a command of the language can expect a beautiful career," I complimented Zhan, hoping to compensate for my earlier rudeness.

It wasn't until after dinner that Zhan and I did talk. Then we talked alone and with an ease and absorption that I think surprised us both. Any aloofness I had observed in his deep brown eyes was gone.

Before Zhan left that night, he asked me to attend Griboedov's comedy *Trouble from the Mind* with him.

"Of course, I would love to go," I said wondering how to explain my mother's rule about chaperones and whether Zhan would mind if Styopa came along. But Styopa had overheard Zhan's invitation and was smiling approvingly, not mentioning a word about chaperones.

"Do you think just this once Momma would mind if I went to the theatre alone with Zhan?" I asked Styopa as soon as Zhan had closed the door.

"Of course not," Styopa agreed. There seemed to be no end to his conviviality. "You are seventeen now, you know."

The alacrity with which Styopa and Maria permitted me to accept Zhan's invitation for a date ought to have alerted me to a conspiracy.

If that were not signal enough, Styopa seemed unable to stop extolling Zhan's merits. Had I heard of the Korolyovs, Zhan's family? They were, after all, one of the best families in Moscow. And what a careful, cultured upbringing they had provided Zhan—"not so easy to achieve these days," Styopa said, permitting himself one of his few critical allusions to the new Communist system. But then Zhan, it seemed, had infinite innate abilities. "Really a brilliant young man." Styopa sighed. "I remember him as a child, always reading—practically a lawyer from birth. The Korolyovs have had lawyers in the family for three generations."

At the theatre the next evening, the audience in the front rows where we sat stared at me. I was accustomed to being recognized in public, but not to this degree. It was only later that I learned that the audience in that section of the theatre was largely made up of

Zhan's fellow law students and that he had informed them that he was bringing "his fiancee."

"For you, Zhan, the play should be entitled 'Trouble from the Heart,' " one of Zhan's friends whispered with a knowing wink during intermission.

From Styopa's excessive approval, I understood that my family was not opposed to my friendship with Zhan. I did not immediately realize that our marriage was nearly a settled matter to both Zhan's and my family.

A few evenings after Griboedov's play I performed at the Bolshoi in the ballet *Red Poppy*, dancing the Chinese dance with Sasha. I was slightly distracted to know Zhan was in the audience. Afterwards he came backstage, bearing a bouquet of red roses. "Would you come to dinner at my parents' home?" he asked.

My mounting certainty that Zhan intended to marry me was confirmed that night at the dinner at his parents' home.

"Ah, Zhan, so this is your Lubasha." Zhan's mother, Maria Ivanovna Korolyova, kissed me when Zhan introduced us.

At the dinner there were the customary Russian toasts. "To your happiness." Viktor, two years younger than Zhan, proffered a toast, clearly including both his brother and me in his wish. Too bashful to propose a toast, the other two members of Zhan's family, Nina, thirty, and Lena, thirty-five, watched me all evening as attentively as an audience at the Bolshoi.

"I hope you will come live with us," Nina whispered when Zhan was helping me into my coat. Zhan scowled at his sister, but Nina's remark left less impression than an earlier event of the evening.

After all the family had proposed toasts, Zhan's father, Fyodor Fyodorovich, had presented me with a platinum watch studded with two diamonds. As he placed it on my wrist, I heard Zhan murmur, "But she doesn't know yet, Father."

"If she doesn't, she soon will," Zhan's father replied brusquely, seeming not to mind if I overheard.

That evening I confronted Styopa with the platinum watch and the conversation at Zhan's parents'.

"Yes, you're going to marry him," Styopa beamed.

"But Momma, what will she say?" I had never expected to

make this decision myself, but I couldn't imagine that my mother would not be consulted.

Styopa pulled a large stack of letters from his mahogany desk. "Momma has known Zhan's family for many years," Styopa announced in the same high, good humor.

Without entirely knowing why, I started to cry.

"But, Lubasha, you do want to marry Zhan, don't you?" Styopa frowned.

I knew that I did. And I had expected and even depended on my mother to choose my husband. But it was so abrupt, not like the languid romances of Turgenev novels.

"And what about Volodia?" I said with a shade of accusation in my voice, suddenly realizing that I had scarcely thought of Volodia since I met Zhan.

"Oh, Momma will talk to Volodia." Styopa flicked away my worries with a gesture.

"Of course you do not have to marry Zhan. It is your choice," Styopa added as an afterthought.

I said nothing, but I knew that Styopa was right. I would not refuse. I would choose Zhan.

Zhan, however, did not formally propose to me until three weeks later on an evening when he had invited me to meet him at a restaurant near the Bolshoi famous for its Georgian cuisine and gala atmosphere. Zhan led me to a table with a large lavender vase overflowing with lilacs and handed me two of the flowers.

There were, I noticed, several places set at the table. "All of our family are coming," Zhan said. "They think that you and I suit each other and should become husband and wife. I want to marry you not only because our parents wish it, but because I love you more than any other woman in the world. Will you marry me?"

I blushed, happy and confused, half-hoping Zhan would prolong his proposal.

But in his usual laconic, legal fashion, he sat back and waited silently for my answer.

I thought of my forgotten passion for Volodia. And what about Zhan? What romances lay buried in his past? In the many novels I had read, matters of the heart were not settled so smoothly. "Have you ever loved anybody else before me?" I now inquired.

Zhan handed me another flower before he spoke. "No, I have never loved anybody else, but I did have a lover. She also danced. She was a Gypsy," Zhan said.

It was not Zhan's Gypsy lover which troubled me. In fact, I scarcely grasped the significance of his confession. Perhaps it was the dignity of truly being the person to make the decision in this momentous matter that motivated me to ask, "Would it be possible, Zhan, for me to think this over and give you my answer in a few days?"

"Of course, Lubasha," Zhan said.

That night I stayed overnight with my sister Ira. We sat in long robes beside an electric heater with shining coils. "You know, Lubasha, it was Momma who knew Valya's parents and thought I should marry him. It is like you and Zhan. Valya and I have been very happy for ten years. I recommend you trust Momma and Styopa."

Zhan, who had been an attentive suitor, a few days after his proposal announced that he would not see me for several days while he prepared for his final law school exams. During those days I found myself missing him acutely. And I also discovered I had no doubts about marrying him. When he called to tell me he had won his diploma from the jurisprudence institute, I offered both my congratulations and my acceptance of his marriage proposal. "So now I will have not only an intelligent, handsome husband, but also a well-educated one," I said.

In June 1933, fourteen months after I had left my mother's home in Kiev, I was sitting with Styopa, Maria, Valya, and Ira at dinner. The doorbell rang in the middle of dinner and Marusia, the maid, plodded to the door.

There in the doorway stood Momma and Dunya . . . without any advance telegram . . . without warning . . . surrounded by suitcases and parcels. We surrounded them, smothering them with our hugs and exuberant exclamations. When we were all settled again around Styopa's table and there was finally a pause in the conversation, I said, "Momma, you haven't asked me one question about my work at the Bolshoi."

"My dear Lubasha, from the tiny fragments you have written, I would have known little indeed." My mother turned to embrace me. "But dear Zakharov has written me in detail and you see, my darling, I know all about you—your work, your behavior, and I am proud."

To me my mother's few sentences were a book of praise, more important at that moment than the most raving review I had received for *Swan Lake*. "I won't change Momma—ever," I promised, flinging my arms about my mother, little realizing how bitterly tested in the future that swiftly spoken vow would be.

Soon after my mother arrived, Zakharov came to call on her. Mother sat clothed in a white batiste gown in the corner of Styopa's parlor. Zakharov came to her, kissed her hand, and my mother nodded graciously. As I watched the scene, my mother seemed to me more than ever the elegant, enthroned queen from my childhood fairy-tale books, and now kind, bald Zakharov was the courtier coming to pay homage.

"Dear Stanislava Frantsevna," Zakharov said, seating himself in a straight-backed wooden chair. "How happy I am that you have come and that you are no longer alone but with your family who need you. And now Lubasha is getting married. How recently she was just a little butterfly," and we all three laughed recalling my childhood role in *Rigoletto*. "But I have not only come to reminisce," Zakharov announced. "I have come to present Lubasha and Zhan with a wedding gift."

Zakharov's gift proved to be the greatest of all possible gifts at that time in Moscow. Through his position in the Bolshoi, he had been able to obtain a place for me in a block of apartments controlled by the Bolshoi theatre.

The apartment building, a twelve-story modern structure situated in the center of Moscow, was reserved only for privileged staff of the Bolshoi. Our apartment on the sixth floor faced Sadovaya, the widest street in Moscow. Besides the scenic view, our apartment had five large and one small rooms; two bathrooms with hot water, shower, and a toilet; two telephones; central heating; and access to an elevator.

With most Moscow families sharing apartments, or at least kitchens and bathrooms, the Bolshoi apartment at first seemed a mirage. But it did not evaporate and immediately our families began to decorate it as a gift which, they insisted, Zhan and I should not see until we entered on our wedding day.

On the eve of my wedding, I sat beside my mother in Ira's

apartment. My white chiffon and lace gown, sewn by my mother's Polish dressmaker on Zagorsky Street, lay across the chair between us. I stared out Ira's window, suffused by a melancholy I could not explain.

Perhaps my mother sensed my mood, or perhaps she had planned all along to have a serious discussion with me before my wedding, which with her usual sense of decorum had been postponed to my last night as an unmarried woman.

"Is there anything you would like to discuss, Lubasha?" my mother asked, her hands smoothing nonexistent wrinkles from my wedding dress.

I had to say something. "I am thankful Zhan is so handsome," I offered.

"I would wish, Lubasha, that Zhan's handsomeness and your beauty would be your least virtues. It is the inner beauty of soul which, I pray, will shine through your outer beauty. Otherwise you will be like a bouquet of exquisite roses in a clay pot. The flowers will wilt and the pot will be discarded, but a beautiful vase will last forever. Spiritual beauty from God is what makes family life happy, and only that will bind you and Zhan together.

"There is one more word of advice I want to give you," my mother continued. "Since you will be a married woman soon, your friends should also be only married people. It is proper." My mother hesitated as if there were other pieces of wisdom she should be imparting, but concluded with a sigh, "What I haven't taught you, life will."

We embraced and, exactly as in childhood, my mother made the sign of the cross over me as we parted.

Nothing, I supposed, could have blurred the bright splendor of my July wedding day. But one slight shadow did cast itself over us. Styopa, my protective brother who seemed sometimes to admire Zhan even more than I and whom I had always expected to lead me to the altar dared not, as a Communist Party member, even attend our church wedding.

My mother had arranged for the wedding to be held at a small church on the edge of Moscow. The church, blue as the spring sky, shabby, and surrounded by birches, was selected by my mother. I was sure she had chosen the church for its scenic setting. At the time I did not consider the advantage of the church's remote location, and so less likely to attract the attention of Communist authorities.

Now fifty years later, memories of my wedding return to me in snapshot sequence, the way they were pasted in my wedding album:

There are the three sleek, black American Lincolns which Styopa had rented from the Metropole Hotel for the wedding party. There is Zhan's father, businesslike as usual, leading me purposefully to the altar. There am I, a princess from a beautiful painting, resplendent in my ivory wedding dress which trails on the green carpet. There is Zhan in a black suit with an enormous white bow tie and white carnations in his buttonhole, looking manly and unshaken. And there is Father Nikolai, the priest, reciting the Orthodox wedding vows as crowns are held over our heads:

> *Blessed are all they that fear the Lord.*
> *Glory to Thee, our God, glory to Thee.*
> *That walk in His ways.*
> *Glory to Thee, our God, glory to Thee.*

5 SOCIETY

Zhan and I knew that our families had scouted Moscow for weeks before the wedding to furnish our apartment. Nevertheless, we were astonished at its luxury when our families escorted us inside the apartment for our wedding reception. Six thick plush carpets covered the floors and decorated the walls. Sturdy furniture was arranged in the living and dining rooms. An antique couch, upholstered with red raspberry velvet, had been placed before the large window that faced Sadovaya Street, the widest street in Moscow. In one corner of the parlor stood a reclining chair, designed especially for ballerinas, which Styopa had purchased for me. On a table beside it Maria had stacked books about ballet and Ira had placed a marquis doll dressed in purple and gold brocade uniform.

For my wedding, Dunya had donned a lilac gown, for once discarding her customary Ukrainian black skirt and white blouse. Now she and my mother stood in my new bedroom in solemn discussion. Later I learned that Dunya had debated for nearly two weeks about where she should hang her wedding gift to me, an embroidered tapestry on which she had begun to work even before she knew that my mother had decided I should marry Zhan. On the tapestry, red and gold threads on black velvet depicted a young nobleman in a fur coat with a raised whip standing in the snow on a moonlit night. Above the scene Dunya had embroidered the words from an old Russian song and added my name: "He's coming, coming to her—his Lubasha." Until the day Stalin's secret police came to take me from my home, Dunya's tapestry hung above my bed.

From the first day of our marriage, Zhan and I enjoyed walking Moscow streets at night. One sultry summer evening we walked along broad Sadovaya where apartment windows stood open to catch the scant breeze.

Slowing from my usual brisk ballerina pace, Zhan and I strolled, clinging to each other and pausing often to kiss. As we stood kissing under a larch tree, we saw silhouetted against the window of a fourth floor apartment another young couple kissing. We paused to stare, struck by this scene, a replica of our own. The couple saw us and pulled apart. The woman stepped out on the balcony and whispered gaily, "Why are you standing there? Don't stop kissing!" Zhan and I laughed. Sadovaya Street had become a lover's lane—a world overflowing with happiness like our own. I doubt we would have believed anyone that night who told us that our world would also experience war.

In 1944, in the midst of World War II, twelve years after our summer stroll, a friend from the Bolshoi called Zhan and me and asked us to come to her apartment to help comfort a young widow whose husband had just been killed at the front by the Nazis.

The widow, whom we had never met before, was distraught, crying, and reminiscing about every blissful day she had spent with her husband. "Our devotion never wavered from the first days of our marriage," she said. "I think there was no other couple in Moscow as fond of each other as we—except perhaps one." And then she recalled a Moscow summer night when she and her husband, kissing before their window, had seen their reflection in another couple on the street below.

Often our acquaintances remarked about the luminous aura that seemed to surround our marriage. "It's like a candle, Luba," one of my ballerina friends warned. "Flames glow, but they also flicker, you know."

On the rare nights when I was not rehearsing or performing, Zhan and I sat in his office, a spacious room with black leather furniture trimmed in gold, and filled with shelves of books. One evening when Zhan sat at my feet, his head in my lap, I reminisced about Kiev and Volodia and my fifteenth birthday party.

"Were you in love with Volodia?" Zhan asked.

"With Volodia and his white lilacs," I laughed.

In the first year of our marriage I awoke on my birthday, April 25, to find an overflowing basket of white lilacs beside my bed. "But where could you possibly find white lilacs in April?" I exclaimed to Zhan.

"They say a man in love can find anything," Zhan said. "You wait and see, Lubasha. I promise white lilacs every year for your birthday."

In this way white lilacs became a tradition of our marriage, reserved only for my birthday. However, a remarkable event at the Bolshoi prompted Zhan to ask my permission to break our tradition.

The occasion was a special performance in honor of a Bolshoi Theatre contralto soloist, Nadezhda Andreevna Obuchova, a singer beloved by all Moscow and especially by the Bolshoi staff. When the Bolshoi announced that Nadezhda Andreevna would present a concert in honor of both her sixtieth birthday and fortieth year as a singer, Zhan, a devoted fan of Obuchova, immediately purchased tickets and pondered how he might honor the famous singer.

"If you would not think me disloyal, Lubasha, I think a bouquet of white lilacs would be the best tribute I could offer Obuchova in December." I agreed, convinced that my clever husband, who could find white lilacs in April, would somehow also succeed in December.

The night of the concert, after Zhan escorted my mother and me to our seats, he hurried to deposit his bouquet of white lilacs in a room next to the stage where he could collect them after the performance and personally present them to Nadezhda Andreevna.

"But, Zhan, what is the matter?" I exclaimed when my husband, with a crestfallen expression, settled into his seat beside me.

"You will never believe this, Lubasha. Among the hundred bouquets in that room, the first one I noticed was another bouquet of white lilacs, even larger than mine. How could anyone else find lilacs in December?" Zhan groaned.

After the concert, determined to salvage what glory remained from his no longer unique gift, my gallant Zhan rushed to collect his flowers and present them to Nadezhda Andreevna.

When Zhan returned, he was accompanied by a man in a general's uniform. "I found the other owner of white lilacs," Zhan announced, introducing my mother and me to Fedor Romanovich

Liputin, who, we learned, was an aeronautics engineer and also a general in the Soviet Air Force.

We joked about the white lilacs, exchanged other pleasantries, and as we left the theatre met Fedor Romanovich's mother, Valya Ivanovna Liputin, a cultured woman with whom my mother was soon conversing enthusiastically.

"People who like white lilacs are bound to discover other common interests," Fedor Romanovich said jovially. "I propose the five of us have dinner together this evening."

That night inaugurated an acquaintance which rapidly blossomed into friendship. My mother and Valya Ivanovna met together nearly every week, and Fedor Romanovich, who was forty-five years old and a bachelor, came often to our apartment.

One day I received a telephone call from Valya Ivanovna. "Luba, could we meet at the Razov coffee shop? There is an important matter I would like to discuss with you."

At the coffee shop Valya Ivanova plunged into what she described as a "painful subject," but one about which she wished to seek my advice. She was terribly worried, she confided, about Fedor, already forty-five and not married. I must know so many lovely young women at the Bolshoi. Was there anyone to whom I might introduce Fedor? I tried to cheer Valya Ivanovna and although inexperienced in matchmaking, promised to try to help.

Two days later, I returned home one afternoon from the Bolshoi to find a letter from Fedor awaiting me.

I tore it open, expecting an invitation to a concert. Instead an impassioned declaration met my eyes. "Forgive me, Luba Leontievna," the letter said, "but I cannot conceal my love for you any longer . . ."

Without even finishing the letter I dashed to the telephone, and when I was sure that Dunya was safely distant in the kitchen, called Fedor's mother. Valya Ivanovna's voice trembled, and I could hear that she was crying. "It is because I was afraid this would happen, Luba Leontievna, that I met with you. I know this event will spoil our entire friendship, and I thought I might prevent it by distracting Fedor with someone else."

That afternoon I sat in my ballerina chair buried in Tolstoy's *Kreutzer Sonata*. But the novel only deepened my distress. After speaking with Fedor's mother, my first impulse had been to phone my mother. But why should I ruin her friendship with Valya Ivanovna? And Zhan—how could I explain this event to him? Perhaps, I convinced myself, if I ignore the letter, Fedor will come to his senses.

But far from retreating, Fedor Romanovich's letters continued, each more supplicating than the last. After the first few unanswered letters, Fedor Romanovich began sending his personal chauffeur to my dressing room at the Bolshoi to deliver his letters. "Shall I wait for an answer, madame?" the chauffeur would always ask.

"There won't be any answer," I would stiffly reply.

Meanwhile Fedor continued to come to our apartment, behaving as usual toward Zhan, but casting amorous glances at me, which I worried that Zhan would detect. Finally after I had received at least twenty of Fedor's ardent letters and could endure the discomfiture of the situation no longer, I resolved to write him candidly and firmly.

I waited until an evening when Zhan had gone on an overnight business trip. I sequestered myself in our bedroom and spread Fedor's letters on a desk before me. I spent nearly an hour composing an answer. "Respected Fedor Romanovich," I wrote, "I have received all your letters and must tell you that if the friendship between our families is to continue, you must stop writing these letters. I love my husband, am fortunate to be married to him, and do not plan to leave him. Your letters are harming not only the friendship between you and me, but among all the members of our families."

I had nearly finished my letter to Fedor when Zhan burst into our bedroom. "The trip was canceled, Lubasha," Zhan announced, greeting me with a kiss. "But I have interrupted you. What are you writing so laboriously?" His hand rested on the pile of papers before me.

Too mortified to reply, I thrust one of Fedor Romanovich's letters into Zhan's hand and watched while he read. To my amazement, his expression registered no reaction. Only his actions were revealing. He ripped Fedor's letter and also my reply. "Let's just forget this whole unfortunate matter, Lubasha, and enjoy an unexpected evening at home," he said, reaching for a Balzac novel which he had been reading.

"But aren't you jealous?" I finally inquired a few hours later in a piqued voice when Zhan, absorbed in his book, seemed to have forgotten the entire incident.

"No, Lubasha, such incidents are best ignored." He smiled and returned to his reading. Rather than feeling reassured, as I suspected I ought to be, I found myself annoyed at my husband's equanimity. If Zhan truly loved me, I reasoned, he would at least be jealous. In fact, he ought to be furious with Fedor Romanovich.

Two days passed with me too proud to again raise the subject to Zhan. By the second day, my tiny doubts about Zhan's ardor had swelled into a tornado of humiliation. The facts, I convinced myself, outlining them as carefully as I had watched Zhan do preparing a legal case, indisputably proved my husband's lack of devotion.

Three nights after Zhan had discovered Fedor's letters, I left our apartment before dinner with no explanation to Zhan and walked to my sister Ira's apartment, where my mother was living. "Zhan doesn't love me anymore, Momma," I sobbed when I had recounted the story of Fedor's letters. "I'm staying overnight. Maybe Zhan will think I am with the general!"

Having uttered this terrible statement, I steeled myself for a stern lecture from my mother. But she, as smoothly as if she had not heard me at all, simply said, "Of course you are welcome to stay overnight, Lubasha. Do calm yourself so we can enjoy the visit."

During that miserable, sleepless night I pulled complaints from a mental briefcase and convinced myself that I had been abandoned not only by Zhan, but by my mother.

The next morning, before breakfast, I crept back to my own apartment. Dunya was serving Zhan's breakfast. He greeted me with a kiss and pulled out my chair. "Do join me, Lubasha."

"Weren't you even worried about me? Don't you want to know where I was last night?" I asked coldly.

"Your mother phoned to tell me," Zhan smiled. And then, as patiently as if I were a child, he continued, "I know you are upset, Lubasha, because I did not react with enraged jealousy. I'm not surprised that another man loves you, but I am terribly proud of the way you refused him for me."

About a week later Fedor Romanovich phoned our apartment. Zhan answered and I heard him say courteously, "Ah, Fedor Romanovich. You will be interested to know that Luba and I will not be at home at this apartment any more," and without waiting for Fedor Romanovich's reply, Zhan hung up the phone.

Early in our marriage another memorable episode unforgettably etched Zhan's devotion to me. One morning as my mother and I sat at the table in our apartment drinking tea, Zhan, his face beaming and a bundle in his hands, burst into the room. He turned the package over on the table and stacks of rubles poured from it.

"It's for you, Lubasha," he said when the table was covered with money. "Spend it as you wish. I won 25,000 rubles* in the government lottery." Zhan, who had always appeared older than his age, was now as excited as a boy at a marble game.

But my mother was horrified. "You know, Zhan, Luba has never managed money," she protested. "She is not accustomed to that." And my mother was right. From childhood to my marriage, I could not remember ever having money of my own. Even after I began to work at the Bolshoi, Styopa managed my money.

Zhan had once again assumed his adult role and now reassured my mother, "It's all right, Momma. Let her spend it any way she wants. Let her learn to manage money." All that evening Zhan proposed tantalizing prospects on which I might spend my fortune— "that painting you saw at the antique store . . . perhaps you want to save it and buy a car." But somehow Zhan's suggestions did not excite me.

My family, who generally strove to insulate me from any unpleasant news of the outside world, had not been able to restrain their anguish at the ravaging famine in the Ukraine, caused primarily by Stalin's drive to force all farmers into Communist collectives. One day I had come upon Dunya weeping and wrenched from her the fact that she feared her people in the Ukraine would starve. In the last months, Ukrainians by the thousands had poured into Moscow. With nowhere else to go, they huddled in Moscow train terminals hoping that some munificent Muscovites might give them money, food, or clothing.

By morning my mind was made up. I stashed the money in the cloth bag I always carried to work. First I went to Kievskaya station, then to Kazanskaya station, and finally to Yaroslavskaya

---

*Approximately 5,000 American dollars.

station, handing out money to the hungry. At first I gave each person several bills, but when I found so many needy people I wanted to make the money stretch as far as it would. People wept and kissed my hands and I started to weep. Once when I thought I might be mobbed with outstretched hands and gratitude, an old man elbowed the others aside. "She's a lady, can't you see. Respect her like a lady."

"No, she's an angel," a woman shrilled who was clutching two children with swollen stomachs and matted hair.

Two militia men, attracted by the commotion, approached me. Politely they asked me to accompany them and escorted me to the main militia station. The officer in charge of the station was stern. "People don't walk around distributing money at railway stations," he snapped, and handed me a questionnaire. Where had I obtained the money? How did I account for my actions?

As noble as Lady Godiva—that was how I had perceived my actions. Now the officer was impugning my honorable impulses, and I began to cry. "I am a ballerina, my husband is a lawyer. We live in a beautiful apartment, and both my husband and I earn large salaries. Since he just won 25,000 rubles in the government lottery, I wanted to share my happiness with others. And is this how my generosity is treated when I try to prevent *nashi*—my own people—from dying from starvation?"

The officer gaped at me for several seconds and then paced the room, shaking his head. Finally he paused before me. "I apologize," he said curtly. "You may go."

Because the police had stopped me before I had distributed all the money, I decided to use what remained to buy gifts—ten pairs of white shoes, all alike, for my ballerina friends in Kiev. With the last twenty rubles, I bought Zhan a necktie that he has kept to this day as a memento of the happy years of our marriage.

A few days after this event, a long article appeared on the third page of *Vecherniaya Moscura*, entitled, "Ballerina Luba Bershadskaya Shares Her Happiness." My colleagues at the Bolshoi posted the article on a bulletin board behind the theatre curtains, where it remained for almost a year.

My mother, who was living with my sister Ira and her husband, Valya, visited at my apartment almost every day. With my schedule of eight to ten hours per day of practice and performances both inside and outside the Bolshoi, I seldom had a free evening. When I did, Zhan and I would often invite my mother to a symphony concert.

Mother would begin to dress for the evening early in the afternoon, considering each piece of clothing in her closet and also from the trunks and suitcases stacked around the room which all contained elegant, pressed, scented clothes, often purchased in Paris, where my mother had done most of her shopping before the Revolution. A bijouterie held brooches, pins, necklaces, and many diamond rings. Brocade handbags, silk handkerchiefs, and expensive furs were stored in a cedar trunk. How could I have known then what I would have given for even one swatch of that warm fur ten years later in a Siberian prison?

On the evenings we attended the symphony, Zhan and I, *haute coutre* ourselves, would arrive early to meet my mother, for whom punctuality was a part of piety. She would be sitting in her apartment, elegant in a long evening dress and fur cape. If I complimented her, she would inevitably reply with unconcealed pride, "Do you know how old this is, Lubasha? I bought it in Paris the summer before Ira was born." Before we left the apartment, Momma would reassure herself with one last glance in the small mirror with a pink rococo border which she always carried in her handbag. The gold-tipped hairpin in the French roll of her hair glinted and gleamed under the light in Ira's hallway.

It was almost always in the taxi on the way to the concert as she was unfolding her black fan with azure roses that my mother would remember to instruct me. "Don't whisper to me during the concert, Lubasha. We will share our impressions during the intermission. Don't laugh loudly, and don't look around." I would nod obediently at the admonitions I had heard since childhood before every concert I had ever attended with my mother.

Though my mother continued to sometimes treat me as a child, she clearly regarded Zhan as an adult, and her esteem for my handsome, chivalrous husband was apparent to all my friends. Zhan, to my delight, was equally devoted to my mother and surrounded her with courtesy. Rather than a simple "pardon me," Zhan with his courtly manners always said to my mother, "Oh, a hundred thousand apologies."

My mother, inordinately impressed as she was with such chivalry, could not resist a moralizing rejoinder and would invariably observe, "Of course, Zhan dear. But better one apology, you know, if it is sincere!"

It was Zhan who initiated the most long-lived humorous tradition of our family. The few evenings I had free to relax in my recliner chair, Zhan would often draw. One evening, talking on the telephone, I noticed that Zhan was sketching me. Not close enough to see the sketch, I finished my conversation, then peered at the paper, preening myself for a flattering portrait. Instead I saw a rabbit, whose face bore a remarkable resemblance to mine, jabbering into the telephone.

I laughed so loudly that Dunya came scurrying from her bedroom shaking her head at the "children's silliness" but unable to resist smiling herself when she saw Zhan's cartoon. Soon the stack of rabbit sketches, which we kept on the table by Zhan's chair, began to grow, all stamped with unmistakable Lubalike expressions and Zhan's succinct inscriptions, "Rabbit combs hair . . . Rabbit dresses for theatre . . . Rabbit chooses hat."

It was as a result of Zhan's portraits that I acquired a new nickname—Zaitsa or Rabbit, a sobriquet soon as much used by my friends as my real name.

"Is Zaitsa at home?" a caller would inquire of Dunya who often answered the phone.

"Luba Leontievna is at home," Dunya, who could not quite bring herself to condone all the frivolity, would stiffly reply.

Ten months after Zhan and I were married, when I was only eighteen years old, my first child was born. Often during the early months of my pregnancy, I stood before a mirror and watched my slender figure starting to bulge. I did not want to stop dancing; I did not want to lose my figure; and I was uninformed about childbirth. It was Zhan who found a physician for me, Dr. Krutza, a gynecologist professor who was a friend of Zhan's family. It was the physician at the Bolshoi who told me I must stop dancing at the fourth month of my pregnancy and not resume until four months after the baby was born.

Now I had time for Zhan and Momma and all my friends, but I also had time to eat and had an obsessive urge for cheese ravioli, of which I must have eaten three thousand before my baby was born.

My brother Styopa, always the jovial one in the family, teased me that I was turning from a giraffe to a cow to an elephant. But Zhan, fearful I would be offended, even abandoned his rabbit drawings during my pregnancy and gallantly tried to console me, saying, "You know, Lubasha, I never imagined that stoutness would be so becoming to you."

Our son Lyonya, whom we fondly called Lyonechka, was born on the eve of my eighteenth birthday. Before the birth, Professor Krutza reassured me, "Don't worry, Luba Leontievna. With your trained ballerina's body, your delivery should be swift and easy." But as it was, my labor lasted twenty-seven hours, with wrenching, unaccustomed pain, and I reacted with screams that shot arrows of agony through Zhan and my mother, who could hear my cries in the waiting room.

After the birth, I was rolled back to the ward which I shared with fifteen other women. Through my drowsiness I heard the women in the ward grumbling about the "screecher" who had kept the whole hospital awake. I couldn't resist a reply. "Let me introduce myself," I said before I fell into a languorous sleep.

I awoke to find Lyonechka, blue-eyed and chubby, nestled at my breast, and I discovered that even ballet had receded from my mind at the wonder of my baby. From his birth Lyonechka, the only baby in both Zhan's and my family, was treated as a marvel to be kissed, hugged, cuddled, and smothered with gifts.

He even left the hospital in style. For this day, Zhan's mother had saved Zhan's own first baby clothes—a lavender bonnet, shirt, and quilt edged with lace. I could not help giggling when I saw little Lyonechka bedecked in all his finery. "Let me introduce you to the 'Queen of Spades,'" I said to the nurses who laughed to see the resemblance to the wrinkled, wizened countess in Tchaikovsky's opera who always wore elaborate lace bonnets to bed.

Zhan escorted me home, and when we opened the door to our apartment I stepped into a garden of flowers—everywhere, even in the kitchen. I ran from one bouquet to the other to read the congratulatory notes—from my family, from my Bolshoi colleagues, from my friends. Zakharov had drawn a cartoon card. A ballerina stood in elegant pose, but at her foot a child tugged with all his might, hindering his mother's dancing.

When Lyonya was six months old, I returned to the Bolshoi,

picking up the pieces of my busy, glamorous life as if there had been no break.

By nine o'clock nearly every morning I was at the Bolshoi. Between ballet performances and social evenings with friends, I spent few evenings at home. But summer meant some surcease in our schedule—a month at a Black Sea resort for Zhan and me; and for Lyonechka and later our two other children, a whole summer at a *dacha* on the outskirts of Moscow, another of the benefits Zakharov had acquired for me through the Bolshoi.

Zhan and I and our many friends would visit the *dacha*—a huge rustic house with twice as much space as our Moscow apartment—as often as we could for long, lingering Moscow summer days that turned into perpetual parties.

At the *dacha* there was a bar built especially for me to practice ballet, and we kept stacks of folding cots for the twenty couples who were our closest friends. On many weekends forty-two adults, besides children, stayed at my *dacha*. During the day we played tennis, volleyball, lotto, croquet and swam in the frigid Klyazma River that wound through the backwoods. But the evenings were best. Circled around campfire embers, we sometimes sat talking all night.

Always the conversation would turn to literature, wandering from Tutchev, to Turgenev, to Flaubert, to Maupassant, to O'Henry. In our group of forty-two, there were always at least ten poets. Those bold enough to share their work were like the Chekhov character who is first commended and then criticized with equal fervor.

Although most of my friends, like Zhan and me, had been married in Orthodox churches and had permitted the *babushkas* in their families to take their babies for baptism, religion was not a subject we could freely discuss just anywhere. In our own circle, however, we felt safe.

One weekend my ballerina friend Zoya arrived at the *dacha* without her Japanese musician husband, Miska. "We've had a terrible fight," Zoya sobbed. Zoya confided the miseries of her marriage to us all, and someone suggested that we hold hands around the campfire and pray aloud.

That evening began a ritual in our *dacha* circle that extended not only to insurmountable problems but also ineffable joys. For these times that demanded more than human expression, our circle would hold hands, link arms, and talk and pray—simple sincere sentence prayers to a God we all believed existed but with whom we did not feel well acquainted. When we prayed outdoors I did not close my eyes, comforted by the large, luminous stars which I liked to imagine lighting an entryway to heaven.

During those camelot days at the *dacha*, the Kremlin and the tyrant Stalin who ruled there might have been a million miles away. In reality, Moscow was only thirty minutes by train from the *dacha*. It was through our friendship with Zina, a colleague of Zhan's and one of our *dacha* friends, that the reality of the Soviet world slowly began to impinge on my Elysian existence.

Zina, whose mother was Russian and father Georgian, was a pixie—petite, dark, and vivacious. As Zina told us her story, I could scarcely reconcile her merriment during the day with the tragic memories she shared around the campfire at night.

Zina's father had died when she was a child, and her mother became an alcoholic. Arriving home from school, Zina frequently came upon her mother slumped drunk and disheveled on the stairway or sprawled on the apartment floor.

When Zina finished secondary school, she took a job as a cloak-room attendant at a movie theatre to support her mother and entered university to satisfy her own greatest desire—education. At the theatre, oblivious to admiring male stares, Zina buried herself in her books as soon as the movies began and devoted every moment not required by her work to her studies.

Like me, Zina had been born on the eve of the revolution. Unlike me, she was a true child of the revolution. She had proudly worn the Lenin pin of the Octobrists and the red scarf of the Young Pioneers. As a teen-ager she had swiftly joined the Komsomol, and during Stalin's campaign to collectivize the peasants Zina had been one of the first to volunteer to assist. Once an old peasant had tried to attack her with an ax when she had threatened to report him for hoarding grain, but even that had not daunted Komsomolist Zina.

"I believe in my Communist Party conscience," Zina repeated stoutly during the first years we knew her.

"Are you saying that conscience can be determined by a Communist Party card, Zinachka?" I once summoned the courage to ask.

"If you want to remain my friend, you may talk about anything but politics," Zina had coldly replied. At the time I thought little of the conversation since by common consent politics seldom entered our *dacha* conversations anyway.

More difficult was the ban on this topic between Zina and her husband, Volodia, who was not a Communist. Volodia, an engineer, was devoted to his wife, whom he had met when she worked as a cloakroom attendant at the theatre. He had first admired her from a distance, then sent her ardent notes and flowers, and finally found courage to ask for a date. Zina had married the young engineer and seemingly politics became a taboo topic between them, although once Volodia had confided to Zhan, "Zinachka will see the light. She doesn't yet realize how uncommunistic she is."

Zina had excelled at law school and for four years practiced law. Intoxicated by the limitless opportunities she saw in the new system, she decided to enroll in the Academy of Foreign Affairs, and from this institution was dispched to England on a government project. Zina invited us all to her gala farewell. She, the hostess, gave the final toast. She spoke passionately about the Communist Party which had provided her, an orphan, opportunity to become a professional person. The next week Zhan and I were among the twenty couples who went to Moscow's airport at one in the morning in freezing February weather to bid Zina good-bye. "Promise you will all come out to meet me in three months when I return," Zina called cheerily as she boarded the plane.

But Zina did not notify any of her friends of her return. I only learned from Volodia that she was back in Moscow several weeks later. Volodia repeated sadly, "She won't see anyone."

Finally we learned what had happened. After three months in the West, Zina no longer believed the Soviet Union was a Communist paradise. "I was living in a delirium, a fantasy," she told Volodia, who, although not a Communist himself, cautioned Zina to be careful about what she said. But Zina, wholehearted as always, would not be silent. She turned in her Communist Party card with the written statement, "I cannot live a deception."

Zina was swiftly pushed off her pedestal by the authorities and, convinced that only arrest could follow, retired to her apartment, where she became a recluse. Through all these traumas, Zina and Volodia withdrew from our circle, and it was only years later that I learned Zina had not been arrested, but had become insane anticipating the arrest she believed inevitable.

6 THEATRE

In 1936, when Lyonya was almost two years old, I saw a notice in the Moscow newspaper *Soviet Art* announcing a competition by the Moscow Cinema Institute to recruit actors.

I had been on the stage as a dancer since I was four, but I had always wanted to be an actress. I ran with the clipping to Zhan, who teased me about being a workaholic. "You are always stretching, Lubasha, reaching for something more," Zhan sighed.

Although more prone to activity than reflection, I realized that night as I lay in bed beneath Dunya's embroidered nobleman that Zhan was right. As envious friends had often observed, I had been blessed with everything—a glamorous, prosperous career; a handsome, devoted husband; and a beautiful baby. But there was some force inside me driving me forward to more success, more acclaim. The other triumphs had come so readily and I was only nineteen. Why shouldn't there be more—many more?

But when I disclosed my ambitions to Zhan, I emphasized the practical. "You know a ballerina can't dance forever—especially one who has children. But for an actress there are always roles."

Zhan accompanied me to the Cinema Institute on Pravda Street to fill out the forms for the competition. Two weeks later, 1140 actors, I among them, filed past the commission for the first selection based on suitable personal appearance for the stage. Three more talent screenings followed. By the final adjudication, Zhan, who had cheered me through all the exams, seemed more nervous than I. At the end of the fourth test, thirteen of us from among the initial 1140 were selected by the Cinema Institute Examination Committee.

Zhan, who liked to win as much as I, applauded my achievement. But as soon as the contest was over his enthusiasm began to wane. "You are committing yourself to four years of study, you realize," he observed one evening after dinner when Dunya had gone to tuck Lyonechka into bed.

"Humph! Four years that 1127 other people would have given a fortune in rubles for," I retorted.

"But, Lubasha, you are already overscheduled with rehearsals and performances at the Bolshoi and concerts with Sasha. Now if you enroll at the Cinema Institute, I will never see you. Will you ever have a weekend free for the *dacha*? And what about Lyonechka?"

"I will eliminate all the outside concerts with Sasha. And I can schedule all my classes at the Cinema Institute in the evenings." In my excitement, it was true that I had not stopped to calculate the strain. "I will manage," I insisted. "I must not miss this opportunity."

But Zhan did not agree, and for the first time in our marriage a barrier arose between us. Soon even other members of our families had begun to notice the tension that was rippling our happy marriage. But my mother did not, as I had expected, take my side in the conflict. "Your first responsibility is to be a wife and mother, Lubasha," she insisted.

To my surprise, Maria Ivanovna, Zhan's mother, who all her life had been dominated by Zhan's imperious father, now defended me. "You encouraged Lubasha through all the examinations, Zhan. It is unfair to discourage her now that she has won." Maria Ivanovna stated my case so categorically that even Zhan seemed reluctant to contradict her, and within weeks I began my classes at the Cinema Institute.

But soon another event temporarily slowed my career. By January 1937 I knew I was again pregnant and although I was forced to stop dancing at the Bolshoi, I continued with my classes at the Cinema Institute nearly to the day my daughter, Ira, was born on August 26, 1937.

Ira with gray-green eyes like mine and a sedate temperament like Zhan's seemed from her first days as content to be with Dunya as with me. I stayed home for four months to nurse and care for Ira but then restlessly returned to both the Bolshoi and the Cinema

Institute, somehow still managing to return home at least twice a day to nurse my baby.

Despite my promises to Zhan not to neglect our family, as soon as Ira was weaned I submerged myself recklessly in my career, rushing home from the Bolshoi in time to hurry to my theatre classes at least four evenings a week. On the evenings I was not at cinema class I often performed at the Bolshoi.

All the Moscow art world, I knew, greatly admired Konstantin Sergeyevich Stanislavsky, the aristocratic founder of the Moscow Art Theatre and also its director. Although I had not met Stanislavsky, I, like all other Cinema Institute students, was swiftly introduced to his philosophy and methods. "We are not here to play the stage but to live the stage," Mikhail Mikhailovich Tarkhanov, my mentor at the Cinema Institute and a devotee of Stanislavsky's methods, would repeat. "Become what you act. The life of man's spirit must be expressed on stage. . ." Steadily Stanislavsky's dictums were drilled into us.

"Sit on a park bench," Stanislavsky had advised aspiring actors, "and watch a child at play. If a child pretends to be a bear, it becomes a bear. Children know how to act."

During the second year of my studies at the Cinema Institute, a competition was announced between our studio and Stanislavsky's. "I want you to win, Luba Leontievna," Tarkhanov said. All of the contestants were expected to read from works by Mayakovsky and Pushkin. I chose four pieces from *Eugene Onegin* by Pushkin and the patriotic poem "Passport" by Mayakovsky:

> *Look at my passport*
> *And be envious*
> *Because I am a Soviet citizen . . .*

When the prizes were announced for the competition, I had won two—first prize for the Mayakovsky reading and third for the Pushkin selections. After the competition, even before the clapping had subsided, a messenger scurried to me and whispered, "Zinaida Sergeyevena Sokolova wishes to see you." Zinaida Sergeyevena Sokolova, I knew, was Stanislavsky's sister, the art director of her famous brother's studio. But hurrying to her office, I could not imagine why she should want to see me.

Sokolova greeted me graciously and announced, "I consider you very talented, Luba Leontievna. A competition is being scheduled in our studio to find a dramatic heroine. I would like you to try out for this. You will be reading before my brother."

Without stopping to be intimidated at the opportunity Sokolova was offering me, I found myself saying, "I would be delighted . . . honored to accept."

"I will be calling you soon to arrange an appointment," Sokolova said, ushering me from her office.

Although my classmates and I could scarcely believe my good fortune, Sokolova did call about four weeks later and scheduled a date for me to appear before her brother. Zinaida Sergeyevena herself met me and escorted me to Stanislavsky's library. As we walked down the corridor she said, "My brother is not at all well. He will not be discussing your readings with you, but will give his impressions to me to convey to you."

I entered Stanislavsky's library with the sensation of approaching a shrine. Stanislavsky sat in an enormous leather chair with a red plaid woolen blanket thrown across his lap. It was his hands I noticed first, the long sensitive fingers of an artist reclining gracefully on the plaid blanket. His voice was feeble and his face fatigued. He greeted me and gestured for me to begin my recitation.

First I read one of Krylov's fables, then a passage from Tolstoy's *Resurrection*, and finally a poem from a favorite author of my mother's, Ognivtsev:

> *O blest deceit! Only*
> *A mother could feign in such a way,*
> *Afraid her son might falter*
> *On the gallows.*

Stanislavsky sat with his head bowed, not forcing me to meet his penetrating eyes.

When I had finished the last line, he beckoned me to him and I knelt before him. "Keep on studying, Golubchik, little dove," Stanislavsky said, stroking my hair.

As Sokolova had promised, it was she who conveyed Stanislavsky's assessment of my performance. "Luba Leontievna's appearance and temperament are right and she has abundant talent,"

Stanislavsky had judged. "But her breathing is wrong. The diaphragm, not the clavicle, should be used in breathing."

"Take one year to learn how to breathe correctly and then return for another tryout," Sokolova advised. But before I could fulfill those instructions, Stanislavsky had died and my career had turned in a dazzling new direction.

One of the actors who was also a consultant at the Cinema Institute was Vladmir Nikolaevich Yakhontov, renowned as the greatest dramatic reader in Russia and perhaps most famous for his recital of Pushkin's *Eugene Onegin*. Yakhontov's director was his wife, Elikanida Efimovna Popova, a gifted woman who was a poet, sculptor, and artist as well as a theatre director.

One day I was sitting in Gorky Park with my sister Ira. Yakhontov, who was strolling by, stopped and spoke to us. We visited a few minutes, and before Yakhontov left he asked for my telephone number.

I, feeling honored that Yakhontov had even stopped to speak with us, readily gave him my number. "You gave your number to him needlessly," Ira scolded with Yakhontov had gone. "You are a married woman, and I don't approve of the admiring way he looked at you."

Two days later Yakhontov called and asked if he might come to my home to discuss a serious project with me. Elikanida Efimovna accompanied her husband, and it was when we all were settled around my table over steaming glasses of tea that Elikanida Efimovna unexpectedly announced, "Yes, I agree with you, Vladimir. You have found Nina." And it was in this manner that I learned why Yakhontov had regarded me so intently in the park. Yakhontov had adapted two scenes from Lermontov's novel *Masquerade* into a drama for two actors for a forthcoming production. For two years he had been searching for the right woman to play Nina, the heroine.

As often as success had tumbled over me like a waterfall, being asked to perform with Yakhontov was a greater triumph than the most ambitious aspirations of any student at the institute, and I was determined not to disappoint Yakhontov who had bestowed such a great honor on me.

Yakhontov and Popova, affable and relaxed on social occasions, strove to excel each other in their commitment to perfection at work, and—I soon discovered—expected the same dedication from me.

Popova, who was later to become one of my closest friends, was particularly intense and once when I laughed at a blunder I had made, struck me. "An actress can't afford to joke about her mistakes," Popova shouted.

Although I was still dancing at the Bolshoi and studying at the Cinema Institute, I now spent several hours a day rehearsing with Yakhontov and Popova, sometimes even over the phone. As the day drew closer for our premiere of *Masquerade*, the three of us spent hours planning every detail of the performance. It was my mother who helped me find the proper costume for my role as Nina—a long, white, lace dress, white gloves, a white feather fan, and a diamond brooch belonging to my mother, which I wore in my hair.

I did not find it difficult to live the part of the beautiful Nina who is married to the rich, handsome, worldly-wise gambler Evgeniy Arbenin. At the time we began to perform together, Yakhontov was forty-two, I was twenty; and not only our ages, but also our temperaments matched our roles. Yakhontov with his low forehead, squinting eyes, and short stature did not seem a particularly heroic figure at close proximity. But his commanding voice and presence suited the role of the strong-willed Arbenin who is twenty years older than his wife Nina.

In the drama, Arbenin wrongly suspects that Nina has given one of two beautiful bracelets, which he had presented her, to another man. This suspicion drives Arbenin to a jealousy, equal to Othello's, and destroys the Arbenins' marriage.

I loved the role of the innocent Nina. But it was the part of the betrayed Nina that I played best. The jealous Arbenin refuses to believe Nina's explanation for the disappearance of the bracelet. Arbenin poisons her food and only at the last dramatic moment, when death throes are wracking Nina, does Arbenin realize that she is innocent.

"I condemn you as a killer," Nina groans.

"What use is there condemning me? God condemns me!" The wretched Arbenin, raving madly, bows over his dying wife. Music composed especially for *Masquerade* by Yakhontov's friend Aram Khatchaturian swelled from the orchestra pit.

Following this final scene, Yakhontov would lift me, the crumpled Nina, and we would both bow to the audience, which greeted us with tumultuous applause and almost always a standing ovation.

Before the premiere and for the three years following that we performed *Masquerade*, my name was displayed across Moscow beside the famous Yakhontov's. How proud I was to see my name, a novice actress, in the same large letters as the famous Yakhontov's! On the night of our premiere of *Masquerade* at the House of Unions Hall, the audience crowded the aisles. But my exhilaration did not subside even after six encores. That evening when the last press interview concluded, Zhan escorted me to our apartment—filled with three hundred red roses from Yakhontov.

One day, when I had first begun to work with Yakhontov, we were standing together near the window in his seventh-floor apartment. "Wouldn't it be terrible to fall out this window," he strangely observed, staring at Pledensky Street two hundred feet below. I thought little of this remark, attributing it to a passing melancholy mood. How could I imagine that in 1945 Yakhontov, my talented teacher and friend, would commit suicide by jumping out a window? It happened after Yakhontov, perhaps the best Pushkin actor in the Soviet Union, had been excluded from the annual anniversary performances of Pushkin because he refused to join the Communist Party.

Unlike me, who buried myself in my career and family and shut myself away from the uncultured Soviet world, Yakhontov was one of the many people in 1937 who joined the crowd which rushed to a newspaper at five o'clock every morning and found themselves mesmerized by the latest lists of arrests of "enemies of the Communist Party and Soviet people."

Zhan too studied the newspaper, but almost never alluded to the terrible events emanating from the Kremlin, less than two miles from our apartment. Like so many privileged people in the beginning of the Stalinist period, Zhan simply refused to believe Russia was being ruled by a madman. Also Zhan, with Momma, Dunya, and Styopa, had joined the family conspiracy to shield me. Although the mother of two children, I was the delicate one . . . the child . . . "the little one."

Although I was aware of the lists of arrests, I almost never thought about them. If I did, I dismissed them with the comforting logic that the victims must have been guilty. Otherwise, how could they have been arrested?

The first time the arrests entered my world in a more personal way was the winter of 1937. It all began with a banquet held in honor of several high government officials returning from an overseas assignment. Both Lazar Moiseyevich Kaganovich and Marshal Mikhail Nikolayevich Tukhochevsky were present, participating in the central event of the banquet, a web of unending toasts to Stalin. It was in the middle of this outpouring of praise to Stalin that Marshal Tukhochevsky stood and startled everyone by proposing a toast to "beautiful women."

When the toasts had ended, Marshal Tukhochevsky asked me to dance with him.

Several months later, Zhan entered our apartment clutching the morning paper. Ashen, he showed me the arrest list which he usually took great trouble to conceal. He pointed to Tukhochevsky's name. Bewildered and more alarmed at Zhan's anxiety than the marshal's arrest, I brushed the news aside. "But, Zhan, what does Tukhochevsky's arrest have to do with us?"

"Don't you remember his toast last winter at the banquet to beautiful women? And then he danced with you." Still uncomprehending I stared at Zhan. "Now they are arresting not only the guilty, but also their relatives, friends, and associates," he said, divulging more to me about political events than he ever had before.

By 1940 I was in my final year at the Cinema Institute and straining to excel at my final project—acting in the movie *Patriotka*, an attempt at Soviet realism with a hackneyed plot which I disdained but knew I must complete for my diploma. In *Patriotka* I was the heroine, riding a horse, retreating from the White Army. There was no way of avoiding the role—I had to learn to ride a horse, coached by my gallant Zhan. But just when the production was ready for filming, I discovered that I was pregnant again. My director dismissed the problem. "So have an abortion, Luba Leontievna. You know it is as simple as buying a bottle of vodka."

The possibility of an abortion had occurred to me, but now I loftily replied to my director, "My mother and Zhan wouldn't permit it. We are not that kind of people."

On June 4, 1941, eighteen days before Hitler marched into the Ukraine, my third child, a son, Vladislav, was born.

7 WAR

On June 22 at eight o'clock in the morning and every fifteen minutes thereafter, the voice of a Radio Moscow announcer boomed through the mahogany case that held our radio alerting us to listen for a major announcement at noon from Vyacheslav Mikhailovich Molotov, Premier of the Council of Ministers. Molotov's words, when they came, were clipped. Russia was at war with Germany. "Our cause is just. The enemy will be beaten and we will be victorious," he declared, leaving Russians who read newspapers to wonder why Hitler, who had signed a nonaggression pact with Stalin two years before, should overnight become our enemy.

On June 23 I walked to the Bolshoi as always, taking refuge in my customary routine. As I walked, a long, black Buick with a Nazi flag, escorted by police cars with wailing sirens, drove past. The German ambassador, wearing a Nazi helmet, was being driven in the limousine to Sheremetyevo Airport, from where he would be flown to a neutral country to be exchanged for the Russian ambassador who was that day similarly being escorted from Germany.

Somehow that ceremony, even more than Molotov's announcement, heralded to me the reality of the war. Nevertheless, I tried to convince myself that surely the war would be confined to a few symbolic conflicts and end swiftly. How far beyond my ballerina's comprehension it was that this war would last five years and result in twenty million Russian deaths!

The same day that Molotov made his announcement, Styopa, who as Moscow's commandant was already a military officer, was sent to command the Russian cavalry in Smolensk. Ira's husband

Valya was also inducted, and in a few days we heard from Dusya in Kiev that her Jan had been sent to the front. Three days later Zhan was summoned before a military commission housed in Octobersky School Number Eight, one of the many public places which had been converted to recruiting centers.

A stream of young men escorted by their families poured into the center. Some, like Zhan and I, clung together. But most of the young men walked alone, with their gaze as distant as if they were already at the battle front. It was the mothers, sisters, and wives who were bent, weeping openly. One young man, smelling of vodka, staggered against me. "Tomorrow I'll be seeing a movie in Berlin," he boasted.

Zhan was summoned into a recruiting room. He returned pale, but in his usual restrained fashion, announced, "Tomorrow morning, Lubasha. I must leave then for my post, and I am not permitted to tell you where I will be stationed. They warned me that I would be subject to military arrest if I revealed the location of our camp," he explained, embracing me and pulling my tearful face toward his, for once neither of us mindful of Momma's rules about public decorum.

"And what about your ulcer? You know the doctor said you must follow a special diet. What if they send you to the front? It's the end of life on earth—at least our life." I wailed as dramatically as if I were reciting lines from *Masquerade* and clung to Zhan.

The next morning when Zhan had gone, I wandered from room to lifeless room in our apartment. The day war was declared, Zhan and I had insisted that Dunya and the children and my mother evacuate to the *dacha*. I prepared a glass of tea and sat in my recliner chair, but found the familiar rituals only a reminder of Zhan. That evening Viktor, Zhan's brother, who was himself scheduled to report for military service in a few days, came to console me. We speculated about where Zhan might have been stationed. "I've heard of a military juridical camp in Zagorsk. That seems a likely place to send a lawyer. And you know, Luba, Zagorsk is only an hour from Moscow," Viktor said.

I lay awake all that night under the stern eyes of Dunya's tapestry nobleman, his uncoiled whip a prod to do something . . . anything. But this crisis loomed unlike any other challenge I had ever confronted. Those had been resolvable with talent, work, or charm. But now the simple pleasure of meeting Zhan once before he was perhaps dispatched to the front never to return seemed unattainable.

By the following morning I had recovered my courage. Zagorsk was, after all, only an hour from Moscow by train from Yaroslavskaya Station. It was true that Zhan was forbidden to reveal the location of his camp, but was I forbidden to inquire about it?

When the train arrived at the little village of Zagorsk my resolve again began to falter. I stepped outside the train station, and in the distance saw the breathtaking domes of Zagorsk's many Orthodox churches—blue and gold, spangled with hope and thrusting toward heaven. Surely God wanted me to see my husband and would help me, I told myself.

In June, the dirt streets of Zagorsk were still muddy and I, staring at the ground to avoid the mud, nearly collided with two soldiers. When I raised my eyes I saw juridical medals pinned on each of their uniforms.

"The juridical military camp," I blurted, "do you know where it is located?"

"You must know such questions are forbidden," the older soldier said sternly.

"But it is so important for me to know," I pleaded, my voice breaking. "It's my husband. I must see him," I wept, first softly but then inconsolably.

Through my tears I saw the soldiers exchange uncomfortable glances. "Go straight along this road—two kilometers. When you reach the forest, you will see the camp," the younger soldier quickly said before both men whirled away and were gone.

I started to run toward the camp, but despite my ballerina strength I slowed to a trot, then a walk, and by the end of the road I was nearly stumbling.

Finally I spied a lone soldier with a bayonet patrolling the zone before me and felt certain I had found Zhan's camp. I sat on the grass, rubbed my feet, and tried to decide how to approach the soldier. He was too far away for me to determine whether he was a man likely to be moved by tears.

What would I do if I were a soldier in battle? I mused. The defensive, timid approach had never been my style. It was the offensive, frontal attack which worked best. I strode forward now and presented myself to the soldier with the bayonet.

"Zhan Fedorovich Korolyov," I announced boldly.

"And who are you?"

"His wife," I replied with the same air of certainty that the matter was settled.

"Your passport!"

I pulled it from my purse.

Without a word the soldier walked away, my passport in hand, toward the telephone in the gate house. For ten minutes, which seemed at least an hour, I tried to look nonchalant in case I might be watched through a telescope from the guardhouse, but inside I churned with worry. Why had the soldier taken my passport? To report me? Perhaps it was only to register me as a visitor. And if Zhan was there, would they call him? Would his surprise betray my unauthorized visit?

Through the gates I saw two men coming toward me—both in military uniforms and with shaved heads. Only as they neared did I realize that one was Zhan, walking slowly, staring at me.

"But how did you get here?" both men exclaimed at once. When I had explained everything, Zhan's friend Igor left us and said, "Don't leave until I return, Luba Leontievna!"

Not wanting to leave at all, I settled with Zhan on a pine-covered knoll outside the gates. As always, I spoke in staccato, exhilarated now by my success at finding Zhan and trying to push from my mind the fact that we must again part. Zhan held my hands. "It's a good thing you came on Sunday," he said. "The chief authorities have left for the entire day."

Before I had to leave, Igor returned with a large canvas bag. "I gathered all the fellows and told them about your miraculous arrival, Luba Leontievna," he said with a slight bow in my direction. "You know, Zhan, if any of the officials learn of her visit, they are likely to court-martial you. But don't worry," Igor reassured us. "We have a plan. This sack contains letters from all of the men to their wives and mothers giving their return address. They might court-martial one man, but they won't punish one hundred and twenty!"

Despite my swollen feet, I now wanted to run the two kilometers to Zagorsk to catch the Moscow train. For Zhan's sake, the sooner I could mail the letters the better. But now with the heavy bundle, every step hurt and I climbed in gratefully when a car stopped to offer me a ride and drove me all the way to Moscow.

In Moscow, thankful for the late June sun, I scurried with my bundle to a dozen different mailboxes and mailed the letters. The next Sunday, when I arrived to visit Zhan the woods outside his camp resembled a picnic grounds—with couples everywhere and baskets of food spread between them.

The Sunday before, I had been too distracted to remember to bring Zhan the medicine he needed for his ulcer. But now I handed the pills to him, with worried inquiries about his health. "You know that Lidia Pavlovna's nephew who has an ulcer was exempted from the military. Why shouldn't they release you?" I argued.

"It is not so simple, my dear Lubochka," Zhan said, releasing my hand to light a cigarette. "Such exemptions are only legally possible if the ulcer is confirmed by an X-ray. If a soldier claims to have an ulcer and the X-ray doesn't confirm it, he could be court-martialed for deception and attempting to evade military service."

For nearly three months, I went to visit Zhan every Sunday and every visit I wheedled him to try to seek exemption on account of his ulcer.

"It's no use, Lubasha. You are exhausting the dictionary to persuade me, but you know you can't."

By August Zhan's three-month training period was ending, and I knew he might be assigned anywhere. Every night I slept with nightmares of him wounded or dead in battle. It was in the long night hours without Zhan when I couldn't sleep that I formulated a plan.

The week before Zhan's training at Zagorsk was scheduled to finish, I decided to call on Ivan Mikhailovich Ramazan, the colonel in charge of military recruitment for Moscow. Soldiers with bayonets ringed the building where Ramazan's office was located but at the fourth control point, when I showed my passport I experienced an unexpected flash of friendliness from one of the guards. "Ah, it is the Snegurchka—the little Snow Maiden," he exclaimed. "I will never forget your magnificent performance, Comrade Bershadskaya!" He himself escorted me to Ramazan's office. "Ballerina Bershadskaya to see you, sir," he announced.

Colonel Ramazan sat behind his desk, reminding me of a mangy tiger ready to pounce. His office was a shambles, his uniform equally unkempt, and his expression glowering.

The tiger stood up, straightened his disheveled uniform, and stepped toward me with a grimace that I supposed was a smile. Then in this scenario, so different from the one I had feared when I had walked into Ramazan's lair, the tiger colonel shook my hand and said, "I am at your service, Comrade Bershadskaya."

I made sure my face was suitably mournful before I asked, "Comrade Colonel, are soldiers at the front permitted to follow special diets for ulcers?"

"Diet at the front!" bellowed the tiger. "We don't send soldiers to the front with ulcers."

I permitted myself to cry. "My husband will probably be sent to the front and he is sick, very sick with an ulcer."

"What is your husband's name?" the colonel snapped.

"Korolyov—Zhan Fedorovich," I replied.

"Why didn't we know about his ulcer?" the colonel shouted.

I cast my eyes demurely to the floor. "My Zhan is a patriot, and he wants to go to the front to defend his country."

The tiger's eyes bulged.

"We need healthy patriots—not sick ones," he roared.

I looked ruefully at the colonel, signaling my agreement with his wise words, but to myself I smiled, "You are such a kind tiger."

The colonel picked up the telephone and thundered, "X-ray Zhan Fedorovich Korolyov immediately!"

With the same sorrowful expression fixed on my face, I thanked the colonel and left his office. "Could you tell me where discharged soldiers receive their documents?" I asked my admirer from the Snegurchka days as I hurried past the fourth checkpoint. Outside, on the street, I waved a perfumed handkerchief and forced a taxi to stop for me. "To Sadovaya Street! If you drive fast I'll pay you double!"

My calculations were all correct. Within two hours Zhan was calling our apartment saying in a bewildered voice, "Lubasha, I don't know how it happened, but Colonel Ramazan discovered that I am ill. He sent me to be X-rayed, and the doctor told me that my X-ray reveals my ulcer. I'm being discharged, and I'm supposed to pick up my documents this afternoon. Pack some clothes for me, and come as soon as you can to meet me at the discharge center!"

In the taxi Zhan methodically recounted the details of his release, but the inexplicability of it all, I could sense, perplexed his lawyer's mind. Nevertheless, in front of the taxi driver I responded only with a stream of feigned exclamations of surprise. Only inside our apartment did I tell Zhan the truth.

Immersed in our relief at Zhan's release we had nearly forgotten our family at the *dacha* waiting with worry, expecting Zhan to be dispatched to the front any day. That night Zhan and I hurried to the *dacha*. As we walked up the dirt path toward the door, billows of laughter from inside rolled toward us, the first merriment I had heard in days. The source of it all was little Vladik, for whom Dunya . had sewn a gown that hung on the baby like Rumpelstiltskin's shirt.

The family was not surprised to see me, but when they saw Zhan, even my well-mannered mother shrieked. Dunya plunked Vladik in his droopy gown into a hammock and ran to hug Zhan. Vladik in all the commotion turned and fell from his hammock onto the floor and started to scream. But the boisterous exclamations over Zhan were so loud that it was a few minutes before any of us heard Vladik.

Although the jubilation of that day subsided, nothing could diminish my joy that Zhan was safe—not even the realization that war was everywhere. Styopa had been promoted to general, and Maria had heard nothing from him for weeks. Ira knew only that Valya had been assigned somewhere in the Ukraine. We had no word from Jan and Dusya in Kiev.

The Cinema Institute had closed in June with the declaration of war, and by November most of the Bolshoi staff had evacuated to Tbilisi. As the mother of an infant, I was permitted to remain in Moscow rather than evacuating with the Bolshoi.

Moscow, always a city of lights to me, had become a dark city of unending night. To foil Nazi bombers, all possible light was outlawed after nightfall—no car headlights on the streets and dark blankets over every window. Once when I was wearing white rubber boots in a rainstorm after dark, a policeman sent me home because the Germans might spot me.

It wasn't surprising that we Russians should attribute frightening powers to the Germans. By September 1941 they had swept through the Ukraine, subduing it in their wake. By September they had also begun to heavily bombard Leningrad, and by December 1941 they were pounding at the doors of Moscow.

In January 1942, I received a summons from the Committee of Cultural Affairs. Since I had not evacuated, the letter informed me that I had been included in the list of actors remaining in Moscow who would be serving the wounded by giving performances in hospitals in the Moscow region.

Zhan and I moved back to Moscow from the *dacha* where we had been staying. Now as often as four times a day the whining wail of the siren sounded to alert Muscovites to bomb raids. If we were near a subway we dove for shelter, but mostly we tried to shut out the sirens, thankful for the diversion and demands of work.

Within a few weeks after war was declared, wounded soldiers from the Ukraine began appearing on Moscow's streets—many without legs and arms, others with gouged eyes and bandaged heads, hobbling, cursing, embittered, and often drunk. Surrounded by healthy, beautiful bodies all my life, I had at first shunned the wounded, frightened by these hordes from a horrible, hideous world I had never known.

Now in the hospital it was not hordes, but helpless individuals—sons and husbands, many younger than my Zhan, who himself might so easily have been lying in one of the beds I now visited.

Like the other performers, I tried to ease their pain by doing what I knew best—dancing, singing, reciting poetry—trying for even a few moments to make them smile or forget and lift them from their misery.

While we tried to distract the soldiers' wounded spirits, a legion of exhausted nurses and doctors bent over their splintered bodies, tearing up sheets for bandages, trying to stretch the scarce medicinal supplies.

When Zhan and I were not at the *dacha* we spent every evening huddled beside the radio, grateful not only for news, but thankful even for the warmth the old mahogany box generated in our heat-rationed apartment. While the radio wove some pattern out of the tangled strands of war, its news was not reassuring. The Germans were in Chimki, a suburb twelve miles from Moscow. When Napoleon had invaded, Muscovites had set fire to the city before subjecting it to the depredations of the enemy. Moscow, we were told in the tradition of Russian warfare, was wired to be dynamited if the Germans entered the city. Hitler too would face ashes before proud Muscovy would bow before him.

8 AMERICANS

It was in October 1942, when all of Moscow was weighing whether to desert the beleaguered city before the Nazis invaded, that I stood waiting at a metro stop after a performance in a hospital. A woman with a bouquet of flowers in one hand and clutching a child with the other stood next to me. I smiled at the pleasant scene they created, so different from the wretched, wrecked bodies at the hospital. The woman smiled back. "Have you heard that Stalin is returning to Moscow?" this stranger said to me.

That night the radio verified the woman's report, and the city's morale lifted. While the papers gushed laudatory editorials about Stalin's heroic return to the endangered city, hope surged through Moscow like a blood transfusion.

Emboldened by Stalin's return, most staffs from foreign embassies returned to Moscow in November 1942. With the return of the diplomatic corps and phalanxes of foreigners who had come to staff the embassies, a shade of gaiety returned to brighten tenebrous Moscow. Foreigners, especially Russia's new allies, the Americans and French, were particularly prone to parties and liked to invite Russians. Inevitably romances blossomed between the foreigners and Russian women.

In November 1942 Zhan and I received an invitation to the wedding reception of my friend Alla Karevena, an actress who was marrying an English army captain, Morris Chapman. At the Savoy Hotel, where the reception was held, I met Lieutenant Colonel Robert McCabe, chief of staff of the American military mission to the

U.S.S.R. I spoke to Colonel McCabe in English, the language my mother had taught me as a child, and before the evening was over McCabe had invited me to interview for a job as a translator for the American Embassy.

That night Zhan and I discussed the prospect of the job until morning. With the Bolshoi evacuated to Tbilisi, I had time on my hands. "It's better to stay busy and not think about the war," I said to Zhan.

However, for once I was the one who considered the political implications. As ignorant as I had been of the news before the war, I had not escaped Soviet harangues against the capitalistic, imperialistic Americans. But that was before the war. Now the Americans were our allies withstanding the Nazi menace. Not as thoroughly publicized but widely known was the fact that the Americans were generously supplying Russia's hungry soldiers and populace with food and the Soviet army with weapons.

"What about our friends? Maybe they will be afraid to associate with me if I work with the Americans," I fretted to Zhan.

"The Americans are our allies," Zhan reminded. "Don't worry about our friends. We won't call them. We will let them call us. Then we won't be endangering anybody."

And thus, before morning I had convinced myself that I was in fact making a patriotic choice in deciding to work for the Americans.

I was assigned to the American military mission headed by General Dean. The chief of the department where I worked was Colonel James C. Crockett, a vigorous man about fifty years old with a rugged visage that reminded me of his famous forebear, the fabled Davy Crockett.

Colonel Crockett's office was housed in Spaso House, the residence of the American ambassador, Averill Harriman, located on Arbat Street. Besides Ambassador Harriman, at Spaso House I also met George Kennan, the assistant to the ambassador, who would later himself become the U.S. ambassador to Russia. Often I brought my daughter Ira to Spaso House to play with six-year-old Jo Kennan under the elm trees in the ambassador's back yard. Of all the Americans I met at the embassy and military mission, the Kennans most assiduously attempted to adapt to Russian life, an effort exemplified both by George Kennan's impeccable Russian language and the large, colorful ribbons which little Jo, like a Russian girl, wore in her hair every day.

The greatest gift from the Americans to all of us Russians who worked on the embassy staff was food rations from the United States which the Americans shared with us three times a month, distributing their food when the shipments arrived as jovially as Santa Claus. For some Russians, the food meant the difference between starvation and survival.

Although all Muscovites, my family included, could now purchase food only with ration coupons, my family fared better than most due to my connections with the Bolshoi. Therefore, I carried all the boxes of food I received from the Americans back to my street and distributed the hams, rice, chocolate, and sugar to the hungry children in my block.

One morning on my way to work at the embassy, I stopped to see a close friend, Galya Kornilov, whose husband, Lev Niko-laievich Kornilov, had been arrested in 1937 for anti-Soviet treason. Galya had been quarantined by many of her friends. Unfortunately, like most of her other friends, I also shrugged my shoulders and agreed that Lev Nikolaievich Kornilov must have been guilty. But I did not, like so many others, stop seeing Galya, who still wept every day for her husband to whom she had been married only four years before his arrest. That morning I discovered a new sorrow eclipsing Galya's life. Her father, a genteel man who had worked all his life as a curator at the Tretyakov Art Museum, was deathly ill. "Sugar, I have to find sugar," Galya sobbed. "The doctor says that is the only thing that will prolong his life."

I cried with her, sorry I had no rations left from the last shipment of the Americans, but promising to share my rations as soon as the next shipment arrived.

It was an American, Colonel Wilmeth, who noticed my red eyes and that morning asked me why I had been crying. "I am so sorry . . . I wish I could help." The kind, shy colonel stood stammering at my desk when I told him about Galya's dying father.

When I finished work that evening, Colonel Wilmeth was waiting for me with a twenty-five pound sack in his hand. "It's for your friend," he said.

When Galya saw the sugar, she wept. Her mother cried, too,

and kept insisting that she must see the kind American colonel who had given the sugar and "kiss his hand."

But Galya, with her husband in prison, knew better. "No, Momma," she whispered, hoping I would not hear. "You know it is not safe. He is a foreigner."

How wise Galya was. Standing there in my fur coat, my husband safe in Moscow, my family safe at the *dacha*, with a job both lucrative and enjoyable, how could I envision all the consequences that association with foreigners would bring to my life—or imagine that twelve years later, after my release from prison, I would again stand in Galya's apartment and hear her tell me how her mother had wept when she died and called my name. "Lubasha—if only she were here. She would find some way to help me. Remember what she did for your father!"

I was still dispatched occasionally by the Soviet Cultural Affairs Committee to entertain wounded soldiers. Most evenings I was invited by Colonel Crockett to accompany American Embassy staff to their social events.

But the convivial Americans did not confine their merriment only to evening social events. One afternoon several of the men in our office decided to watch an American war movie and invited me to join them. They sat on the back of their chairs, munching apples and joking. One sentimental scene depicted a regiment of soldiers waving good-bye to their girlfriends at a railroad station and singing, "Don't sit under the apple tree with anyone else but me." Boisterously the Americans belted out the tune and were urging me to join them when Ambassador Harriman, disturbed by all the noise drifting to his office, poked his head in the door. Like lightning, the men dispersed, leaving me to chuckle at the Americans' affable ways.

But perhaps the most poignant characteristic of the Americans was their succession of romantic attachments to Russian girls, escapades in which I swiftly became their confidante, almost every day changing ruble notes into ten-kopeck pieces so their girlfriends would have change with which to call the Americans from pay phones. Frequently, the grateful American suitors brought me flowers as a reward for my assistance. I would protest at the bouquets overflowing my desk and tease the romance-stricken soldiers that I would be "equally pleased with a bunch of grass. You should save the flowers for your girlfriends!"

How many mornings I stood about my desk bandying jokes and nonsense with the lighthearted Americans, little knowing I would pay with months in prison for every hour of this merriment. But it was the girls who fell in love with the Americans and tried to marry them who were treated as the real traitors. There was Lieutenant Leon Jones in love with Valia, who was arrested before the wedding could take place. There was Tania whose affection for an American lieutenant cost her ten years in prison. Then there were Ira and Lila who did manage to marry their heroes only to discover when the war ended that the Americans were no longer allies. "Why did you make friends with foreigners?" Lubianka Prison interrogators would repeat the same question a thousand times to the girls. To the simple truth, "I loved him," the interrogator would lash, "You political prostitute."

One summer day in 1943 some Americans with whom I worked invited me to drive with them to a suburb of Moscow, Cebreni Bor, only two kilometers from Stalin's *dacha*. Every ten yards a policeman stood demanding to check documents—but only my Russian documents. He did not question the Americans who were dressed in U.S. army uniforms. The next time we picnicked in that place, my American companions dressed me in an American army jacket and hat. The somber Soviet guards, to the Americans' glee, waved us through.

Would I have behaved differently had I known the danger lurking for me in such escapades? By 1943 the mere mention of Stalin, Russia's epicenter, made many strong men quake. But I did not know those people. The Americans, now my closest friends, were not accustomed to groveling before dictators.

The two times in my life when I personally saw Stalin were in the company of Americans.

The first time was at a play in Stanislavsky's Moscow Art Theatre. Stanislavsky, an aristocrat and artist, had preferred only classical drama in the precincts of his theatre. But even Stanislavsky's famous theatre could not escape the noose of Communist control which choked art in the Soviet Union by inserting Socialist realist plays into every repertoire.

Therefore, in the winter of 1943, the propagandistic play *Kremlin Chimes* by Pogodin premiered at the Moscow Art Theatre. The entire staff of the American military mission obtained tickets and as usual I accompanied them.

The lights out, the performance about to begin, a floodlight drew the audience's attention to the gilded loge closest to the stage. In an instant the audience was standing, clapping feverishly while Stalin and his retinue entered the dictator's stall.

When Stalin was ensconced in his loge and the audience re-seated, the play began, a dull discourse which even Moscow Art Theatre actors could not enliven.

But the real drama that night occurred when the young actor from Georgia, Mikhail Gelovany, appeared onstage in his role as Stalin. While allusions to Stalin, if not actual roles representing him, were almost obligatory in many Soviet plays of this period, nobody envied the young actor forced to perform that role before the dictator.

When Gelovany stepped on stage, a hush of horror swept the audience. It was Stalin himself who snapped the tension with a loud laugh of what sounded like honest enjoyment at this depiction of himself. A tinkle of timid laughter from the audience politely ensued, liberating poor Gelovany to conclude what must have been the most fearful night of his career. "Is it possible Stalin knows what a ludicrous creature he is?" one of the Americans sitting next to me whispered.

My second encounter with the pompous, pock-marked emperor was New Year's Eve, 1945. In December Colonel Crockett summoned me to his office and announced with considerable excitement that he had just received an invitation from the Kremlin. "It's for a New Year's Eve celebration with Stalin. Apparently they are inviting representatives from all the foreign embassies. They have sent fifteen passes for us and I will insure, Luba, that one is reserved for you. I'm afraid it won't be possible to obtain one for Zhan."

My thoughts, I must admit, were not preoccupied with an audience with the great leader. My greatest concern was what I would wear. White, I knew, was the traditional color for women to wear on New Year's.

Zhan, Dunya, and even the children lined up at our apartment door as I left for the party that New Year's Eve. My off-the-shoulders dress of white Japanese silk fitted me tightly to the knees and spread in full ruffles below. I wore a corsage and matching headpiece of red roses from Zhan. "I like the roses in your hair best, Mamochka," little Vladislav whispered as I kissed the children good-bye before Zhan helped me into my ermine cape.

Colonel Crockett ushered me into a long black limousine with a small American flag on its hood, and in moments we arrived at the nearby Kremlin Spassky Gate. Inside Grigorevsky Hall, servants swiftly appeared to escort us up a long marble staircase carpeted in red to a banquet hall.

At 11:55, the guests, three hundred of us, were summoned to our tables, and I, one of the few Russian guests present, found my place with the Americans. At midnight Stalin, who seemed even shorter than the night I had seen him from a distance in the theatre, entered the room attired in his usual drab military tunic. I could not help comparing his attire with the elegantly dressed guests who had been instructed in the invitation that formal wear was appropriate to the occasion. Stalin raised a glass of champagne and in Russian heavily tinged with his native Georgian proffered a toast to "peace and friendship to all the nations of the world." Immediately after his toast, he left the party.

Since social events were part of my duties as a translator, Zhan was almost never invited to accompany me. My boss, Colonel Crockett, almost always did. One evening as we entered a reception at the Chinese Hall, we passed a group of well-dressed Russian men. One remarked as I walked past, "Look, even among the foreigners there are beautiful ladies."

I stopped to glare and retort in Russian, "And if I am not a foreigner?"

The Russian who had spoken stepped forward and with an elegant bow, which I interpreted as an apology for his rudeness, asked me to dance. Feeling I would be rude to refuse, I agreed.

When I returned from the dance, Colonel Crockett steered me to a secluded corner. "Don't ever dance with those kind of people," he commanded. "But what kind of people do you mean?" I asked. "Just believe me, Luba, you should never dance with them," Colonel Crockett repeated, inviting me to dance with him and shooing the Russians away when they tried to approach again.

President Roosevelt's death in April 1945 was marked by a great outpouring of grief among the Americans in Moscow, who hung their flag at half-mast and imported black cotton to sew arm-bands for all the American embassy staff. A little less than a month later, the Americans were still wearing their mourning bands when victory over the Nazis was declared by the Allies on May 8. That day I joined the jubilant crowds thronging the American embassy.

The Americans hung out embassy windows, exchanging hand-blown kisses with the vast crowd of Russians filling Gorky Street.

Of course, I too was grateful that the terrible war had finally ended. But the conclusion of the war also meant the departure of almost all my friends from the American military mission, and for that I was sad.

To my delight, Colonel Crockett did not leave Moscow until ten months after the war ended and was able to keep me on his staff. The Sunday before his departure in February 1946, he invited me to dinner at the Arbat Restaurant. "I wish I didn't have to leave you, Luba," he said. "I am terribly afraid that you will be arrested as soon as I leave."

"But why?" I exclaimed. "How could I, a totally innocent person, possibly be arrested?"

Patiently Crockett tried to hammer one hole in my colossal carapace of political ignorance. "It is not because you have actually committed a crime," he explained, "but that will be the excuse. Do you remember that night I told you not to dance with those Russian men at the reception at the Chinese Hall? I warned you because they were MGB, secret police. So far I have been able to protect you, Luba, but when I am gone, what can I do? If you are arrested, I will feel responsible for ever having hired you in the first place."

"But I wanted to work at the embassy," I reassured Colonel Crockett, feeling it my duty to cheer him from his morose mood. "Don't worry. I am innocent. Why should I be arrested?" I repeated blithely, not dreaming of the scene that would occur sixteen months later when Crockett would unexpectedly return to Moscow.

At that time, as always, he would stop his car on Sadovaya Street below my apartment and honk his horn three times, as he customarily did to signal his arrival. But I, already in Lubianka Prison, would not be able to answer his summons. My frantic mother would run to the balcony and cross the fingers of one hand with those of the other to depict a mesh prison fence. By the summer of 1947, that was a signal which both my family and Crockett—who had always been wiser than I in the ways of the Soviets—fully understood.

9 ARREST

On March 21, 1946, about a month before my thirtieth birthday, I was alone in Moscow. My mother, Dunya, and the children had all gone to the *dacha* for the week and Zhan had decided to visit them overnight. I decided to attend the premiere of *Vain Precautions,* a new ballet from Georgia. For March, Moscow's weather had turned surprisingly warm, and after the performance I strolled along Petrovka Street, retracing the route Zhan and I had often followed on our evening walks before the war had come, halting that pleasure along with so many others.

Now the war was over. Styopa and Valya had both returned home unharmed, but Jan, my brother-in-law in Kiev, had been killed at the front. During the German occupation of Kiev my sister Dusya had died. Nevertheless, despite these terrible tragedies, my family had been only grazed compared to the gaping wounds of many families decimated by the war. True, the departure of Colonel Crockett and the Americans had been a kind of bereavement to me. But to offset that sorrow, I had the great consolation of my mother, Dunya, and the children living again in Moscow, safe at last from Nazi bombs.

And I, not yet thirty, also had my career. After five years of only sporadic dancing and occasional practice sessions at the bar at our *dacha,* I could not return to the Bolshoi as a dancer, but I would remain with the theatre as a ballet teacher. And then there was my new diploma from the Cinema Institute. As an actress, my career had only begun.

Why then, I wondered, as I changed into a Japanese silk brocade robe, a gift from Zhan, did I that night have such a sensation
of foreboding? A spring sprinkle trickled at my bedroom windowsill.
I shut the window and lay on my bed, my mind a muddle. Maybe
it was Colonel Crockett's warnings from a month ago clinging to me
as gloomily as graveclothes. But if I had not taken his fears seriously
then, why should they trouble me now?

Without bothering to remove my robe or even switch off the
light, I dozed into a turbulent sleep. I was awakened at two o'clock
in the morning by the shrill sound of my doorbell.

"Zhan . . . Momma . . . the children. Something has happened
to them!" I stumbled to the door where someone was ringing the
bell so insistently it sounded like a siren.

By the time I reached the door, I had awakened enough to
call, "Who's there?"

"Open up!" A shout as shrill as the bell reverberated through
the door.

"They'll wake every neighbor on this floor," was my first
thought. "Why should they be checking my documents in the middle
of the night?" was my second.

I started to unlatch the door, but before I had pulled it fully
open, two MGB secret police and a soldier with a rifle leveled at me
rushed into the room. A bedraggled, bewildered man, whom I recognized as our street cleaner, trailed behind.

"Your passport!" ordered the policeman in charge, comporting
himself with the swagger of an army general. I fumbled through my
purse, trembling at the soldier's rifle following my slightest movement as closely as a theatre floodlight.

But the MGB "general," obviously the leader of this operation,
didn't have time for such trifles as passports. Documents had only
been a pretext to enter my apartment. Now, without troubling to
open the passport I handed him, he brandished a piece of paper with
two purple stamps before me. "You're under arrest!" the "general"
announced as triumphantly as if he had just vanquished an enemy
squadron. "You will sit down and not disturb us," he commanded,
pointing me toward my bedroom.

I crumpled onto my bed, the soldier shadowing me with his
rifle. Stationing the street cleaner beside the soldier, the two MGB

men tore into a search of my apartment. Through the drawers, behind the drapes, under the mattresses. Now they were thumping Vladislav's toy bear—who knows what state secrets might be concealed in its stomach! And then Dunya's tapestry, lovingly placed on my wall after days of deliberation, was ripped down with a rudeness that left a tear by the coachman's feet.

Perspiring from battle, the "general" and his aide hurtled feverishly from one closet to the other. Now the MGB marauders were pillaging the kitchen cupboards. Next they were tearing umbrellas from the hallway rack, dismantling their handles.

When the two MGB men left me, the street cleaner, and the soldier together in the bedroom, I tried to ask the soldier a question. But I pulled the wrong string on the marionette. "Silence! You are under arrest!" the soldier shouted, poking his rifle in front of my face while the shivering street cleaner, who had been summoned by the MGB as a witness, cringed beside him.

After four hours the policemen's curses swelled. They had lost the battle—having found not one shred of evidence. Around six o'clock I heard a yelp of victory. The two policemen marched triumphantly to my bedroom, their booty in hand. I strained to see what they held. Zhan's rabbit sketches! A surge of relief welled within me. Now they would understand. This whole ludicrous evening would unravel for the farce it was, and maybe I would even be able to fetch a laugh when I recounted the whole incredible episode to Zhan. But the triumphant "general" was not laughing.

"These codes." He shook the stack of cartoons in my face. "Decipher these for us!"

"Codes?" I repeated incredulously. Surely the man must be joking, but if that were so, why was he scowling so hard? I stumbled on, feeling as if I were pulling a blind man through a maze. "Surely as you can see, these are cartoons . . . They are caricatures of me . . . A joke my husband has created . . . It was his hobby," I added helplessly.

But even as I spoke, the "general" snorted disdainfully. "Rabbits! American espionage! Secret codes! Any fool can see that's what it is," he announced smugly, handing the stack of cartoons to his assistant. "Wrap them carefully," he instructed. "The bosses will decipher these."

The two MGB police returned to their search, their swearing

abated. Now their pawing through cupboards and closets was only perfunctory. The battle had been won, the "evidence" unearthed.

At eight o'clock that morning, the "general" ordered me to dress. "You're coming with us," he barked, stationing the soldier directly outside my bedroom door.

I dressed as painstakingly as always, assuring myself as I did that the police at headquarters, where I was surely being taken, would understand. The nightmare that had just happened was a play. Now the performance was over. Now I would be meeting sane people and Zhan should be back by that evening and would explain everything. If only I could reach him now.

I emerged from my bedroom attired in a gray fox fur coat and black hat—a velvet one with a wide brim and ribbons that my mother had always admired.

The MGB men stared at me; even the "general" was struck speechless. It was the street cleaner who led me back to the bedroom and through my state of shock removed my hat and placed a woolen scarf in my hands. The hat—my mother's favorite—lay woebegone on the bed. "Don't mention any of this scandal to my mother," I whispered to the street cleaner. "Tell Zhan when he comes, but don't say anything to my mother. I'll be back in a few hours," I continued, but the street cleaner was hurrying me back toward my impatient captors.

"The prisoner is permitted to take one change of underwear and six sugar cubes," the "general" announced in a stentorian voice.

"The prisoner!" I exclaimed and started to protest, but the street cleaner had again taken my arm and was now steering me toward the kitchen. "Go . . . go quickly. Find the clothing and the sugar!"

In a sleek car, not unlike the American embassy limousine which had been at my disposal for the past four years, my MGB captors escorted me to Lubianka Prison, the black marble headquarters of the MGB, a building often admired for its architecture by tourists with even less notion than I of the horrors going on inside.

Their foray finished, the two MGB officers deposited me with a guard, who immediately escorted me to a room to be fingerprinted. For the first time during that fateful day, I wept. "Fingerprinting is for thieves," I choked.

"This is not a prison for thieves. This is a political prison for criminals equally dangerous," came the guard's reply, as corrosive as the odor of the fingerprinting chemicals.

Two women guards led me away to another bleak room. "Body search!" one snapped, yanking my fox fur coat from my back. The other woman caressed the russet woolen skirt and sweater which I wore underneath. Mechanically I had donned the same outfit I had worn to the Bolshoi Theatre the night before. I thought of the Bolshoi and the many times Tanya, my attendant, had helped me dress for performances—styling my hair, applying the last strokes of makeup. Now while I shivered in my silk slip, the snappish woman's hands roamed across my body. I jerked from her grasp. "I want . . . I demand that my husband be notified this minute!"

In seconds the guard whirled me back into position and with a guffaw as coarse as her hands chortled, "You won't be seeing your husband—or anybody—for a long time, sister."

"What do you mean?" I cried. But the two women had completed their search and were pushing me like a can on a conveyor belt out their door toward a male guard.

"Quiet. Solitary prisoners must not speak." The guard who had admired my russet suit now put a finger to her lips in warning. The male guard who collected me at the door neither looked nor spoke. With his clanking keys providing our only conversation, I followed him down the dusky corridor, past cell doors showing no sign of life inside.

The guard halted before a black iron cell door, distinguished from all the others only by the small number 22. Without a word, he motioned me inside.

As a child I had read and reread a Russian fairytale about a little girl kidnapped by goblins—banished to another world until a prince came to rescue her from her evil captors. I had cried and dreamed about goblin kidnappers, ecstatic to waken in the morning and discover my mother and Dunya and my world still intact.

Now the fantasy had become the reality. The goblins had finally come, and I was the little girl in solitary cell 22 with only a narrow iron bed, a wooden table, and a stool for companions, filling my hours with bewilderment and tears at my fate.

But even evil goblin worlds settle into a ritual, and by the first day the dungeon dullness of mine was established. At 5:30 in the morning I heard the thump of the guard's nightstick on the wall, the signal to be out of bed in fifteen minutes. Then came the swift escorted trip to the toilet, carrying the pail that served as a toilet during the rest of the day, to be emptied in the foul-smelling bathroom. On good days I could hope for a twenty-minute stroll in the prison courtyard in the afternoon, with my hands clasped behind my neck and my head on my chest, in the concrete prison courtyard.

But during every day there were all the miserable minutes from six in the morning until eleven at night when the boundaries of my world closed to pacing the confining cell or sitting straight on the stool—a slouch against the wall an offense certain to bring the guard with a volley of reproaching raps on my cell wall.

But the scolding was never delivered with words. The rule in Lubianka's bizarre world, I discovered from my first day, was silence purposely broken only by interrogations in order that words there might become lethal in contrast to their impotence everywhere else in prison.

It was not that there was much temptation to make conversation. Besides the mute guards and haranguing interrogators, I saw no one. Like handicapped persons, the guards deprived of speech had developed other means of communication, employed chiefly to insure that a prisoner in solitary confinement should never meet another of his or her own species. In Lubianka, guards communicated with each other by tapping on belt buckles with their keys—a prison Morse code. In other prisons, such as Lefortovo, a cabalistic code of flags signaled by a guard more skilled than most midshipmen indicated when the prison deck was clear.

For the first four days of my new life, I "thawed"—a piece of prison jargon I would later employ myself to describe the slow entry from numbness to feeling after a first arrest. On the fifth night—at two A.M.—the guard summoned me for my first interrogation.

After the nightmare in my apartment, I should have known what to expect. However, with my same abysmal inability to fathom what was happening, I instead actually experienced a surge of hope at the summons. The MGB police who had searched my apartment, for all their self-importance, had obviously been lackeys. Now I would be talking with the bosses. Certainly they would be reasonable. Perhaps I would be permitted to see Zhan and my mother. No, I wouldn't ask to see my mother—just Zhan. How could my mother survive seeing me in prison! For her sake, I would wait a few days until I was sure I would be released.

My interrogator, Nikolai Semyonovich Vestov, was a strikingly handsome man whom I might have expected to encounter at a theatre party. Now this misplaced person stood behind his desk, adding another stroke to the Alice in Wonderland world into which I had fallen.

But it was soon apparent that while Vestov's appearance might have been incongruent with his surroundings, his mentality matched the setting perfectly. "Luba Leontiyevna Bershadskaya. Ballerina. Arrested on grounds of spying for the Americans," he recited.

"Spying for the Americans!" I shrieked. When the MGB had uttered that nonsense in my apartment, I had been too stupefied to do more than mumble. Now I was incensed.

"Nothing will help you if you try to deny your actions," the interrogator said, his voice as controlled as mine was untrammeled.

"Show me the proof!" I cried.

"We have more than enough evidence to convict you," he menaced, waving Zhan's rabbit sketches.

"I demand to see my husband," I said, my courage dissolving in a stream of tears."

"You demand," Vestov sneered. "Political prisoners are not permitted visitors."

And so began nine never-ending months in Lubianka Prison, one day like every other except for Vestov's infrequent interrogations—always in the middle of the night—an interruption which I eventually almost came to welcome as a break in the monotony of my existence. But the interrogations followed their own repetitious litany.

There were always the same accusations. I had worked for the Americans. Therefore, I was an American spy. The main hinge in my criminal case, it seemed, were the rabbit sketches.

As the first weeks passed, I began to mark the progress of my interrogations by the wear on my sketches, those pictures of happiness now smudged and torn, mauled by investigators and held before my eyes at every interrogation session as incontrovertible evidence of my guilt. And because I would not concede guilt, I was the irrational and insane one, not the beast before me trying to wring evidence from the necks of my poor rabbits.

After the first session I did not raise my voice and in fact seldom spoke. What use was speech in a world where words had no meaning? And worse than that, a world where words had not only lost meaning, but were fraught with hidden traps and terrors. Without language, a lost, hunted victim, my last resort was tears.

At most sessions Vestov, who seemed to admire his voice as much as his appearance, seemed not to mind my silence and tears. But there were other days he would try to taunt me to confess.

One day he sneered, "You're guilty, and if you think you can escape by not confessing, you're wrong. As if you matter. It is the will of the MGB that matters, nothing more," Vestov snarled, for once speaking the truth.

"Do you have a family?" I asked after several seconds of silence.

"I have a wife and a little daughter," Vestov said, straightening his shoulders proudly and, to my surprise, permitting the discussion to deviate from my guilt.

But I was the one who brought the subject back to the prison. "Poor little daughter to have such a father," I said.

"You political prostitute. You'll be sorry for those words!" Vestov lashed, pressing a bell for a guard to lead me from his room. But that day, full of deviations, held yet another surprise. Today there was a new guard. Usually the silent guards seemed as similar to me as a set of identical toy soldiers Zhan had bought Vladislav. Like the toys, my martinets never spoke, but marched me to my cell in surly silence, averting their eyes or clutching their nightsticks if I looked at them. This day, through my tears, I stared at my new guard. He lowered his eyes as he unlocked the door to my cell, but stepped inside and paused a few seconds. "When will people stop torturing people?" he mumbled—daring words that could have cost him torture.

The guard's question, of course, was the one I could not answer. Nevertheless, I turned it over in my mind night and day in much the same manner I could recall Dunya examining a piece of cloth at the marketplace, holding it up to the sun, pulling it, running her fingers across it.

But there the similarity ended. Dunya would not have lingered all day at the market. For me in my constricted cell, there was nothing to distract from my endless cross-examination.

The only patch of beauty in my dreary cell was a glossy parquet floor. How inordinately cheered I had been that first day by this one fragment that would remind me of my former life. But by the next morning I had discovered my captor's demonic ability to convert every solace, no matter how slight, to torment. Beside the bowl of breakfast gruel a guard shoved through my door that first day lay a large ball of cotton. I could not fathom what it was for until an hour later when the same guard swung open my door and shoved the cotton into my hand and me to my knees. When I still stared, he grabbed my hand with the cotton and bent me to polish the floor with the cotton.

Now the tedious, tiring morning chore had become another rung in the ladder of each unbearable day. On my knees, and with hands which Momma and Dunya had never permitted to wash a dish, I rubbed the parquet floor until my body ached, fearful my twenty-minute outdoor excursion would be rescinded if the gloss did not please the guard. To deaden the agony of this hated daily chore, I permitted myself a luxury I feared I could indulge in without losing my mind. Every morning as I rubbed, I would think of my family: one hundred strokes while I thought of Zhan, one hundred for Momma, and seventy-five for Dunya and each of the children.

During my sixth month in the Lubianka, Vestov shunted me to a new interrogator. "Take her up to the ninth floor," Vestov ordered my tacit guard.

But before we reached the ninth floor, the guard halted beside a door and motioned me inside. Breaking the rule of silence he commanded, "Comb your hair. You're going to stand in the presence of the general."

I stood before the mirror, the first that I had seen since I entered the Lubianka, and stared at the stranger in the mirror with straggly hair, haggard face, and haunted eyes. A lot of good it will do to comb my hair, I thought ruefully as I saw in the mirror my russet skirt and sweater which I had worn since I entered the Lubianka, now turned to a gray and grimy rag.

When my guard had delivered me to the ninth floor, I shuddered to discover that my new interrogator was an old acquaintance— General Leonid Fedorovich Reikhman, the husband of Olga Lepeshinskaya Keroween, second ballerina at the Bolshoi and my colleague. I had heard macabre stories about Reikhman, the Director of the Counterrevolutionary Department; but, as I did with most unpleasantness in those days, I had largely discounted the stories as gossip. One of the rumors, I now recalled, was that Reikhman's favorite game as a child had been strangling cats with the shout,"Death to the enemy!"

It was through Colonel Crockett that I had begun to believe the stories about Reikhman. One evening in 1945 I had accompanied Crockett and a group of American army officers to the ballet *Red Sails.* That evening, Olga Lepeshinskaya was the soloist and Reikhman, dressed like a grandee from czarist days, had entered a well-guarded loge near the stage. "That is Leonid Fedorovich Reikhman, the husband of Olga Lepeshinskaya," I whispered to Crockett, who I knew was always curious to identify Russian notables.

With a scowl Crockett said, "He's an MGB general. Stay away from him, Luba."

Now as the door slammed behind me, I did not have that choice.

"Luba, sit down." Reikhman, standing before me, greeted me as congenially as if we were both at one of the many parties where our paths had crossed. Six months in the Lubianka had made me cautious, but it was only human to hope. Maybe Reikhman wasn't the devil Moscow rumor said. Nevertheless, Crockett's warning hovered in my mind.

"Sit down," Reikhman repeated. Stubbornly I stood.

"Sit down!" Reikhman snapped, all cordiality vanishing from his countenance.

"I said sit down." Reikhman stood beside me now, a snake coiled to strike.

I stared at this reptilian creature and, before I had considered what I was doing, spat at him, full in his face.

Reikhman, stunned, stepped back, pulled a linen handkerchief from his pocket, and carefully wiped my saliva from his lips.

"Take her away!" Reikhman ordered the trembling guard.

It was not until a few months later that I learned from other former Lubianka inmates that Reikhman's restraint that day had not been typical. His usual style, I was told, was to burst in on an interrogation already underway and jeer, "Why are you still wasting your time with that prisoner? I thought you had sent him to hell long ago!"

After I had been transferred from the Lubianka, I met Tatiana, an actress arrested for her association with an American. Her experience was characteristic of the consequences of challenging an interrogator.

At Tatiana's interrogation, the investigator had taunted, "What could a beautiful woman like you find in that ugly American?"

"So what if he is ugly. At least he is not a Soviet man," Tatiana had sneered.

"I'll make you pay for that," the investigator snarled and he had kept his word. Tatiana was taken to a punishment cell the size of a telephone booth, whose walls were coated with frost. Tatiana, naked, was shoved inside. When she lost consciousness, she was revived by a guard pouring cold water over her.

After my encounter with Reikhman, Vestov's interrogations became almost perfunctory. It was in November 1946 that I was summoned to Vestov's office for what would be my final interrogation. "Your interrogations are complete, Prisoner Bershadskaya," Vestov announced. "All that remains is for you to verify the evidence," he said, handing me a folder with the title, "Paperwork Related to the Interrogation of Luba Bershadskaya."

I leafed through the papers. There were transcriptions of all my interrogations by Vestov. Also in the folder I discovered transcriptions of Vestov's conversations with twenty-one of my friends who had been summoned for interrogation, but of course never permitted to speak to me. Starved for even this contact with my friends, I hungrily read each word of their interrogations. Vestov had asked every person the same senseless questions. The answers, extracted separately, nevertheless all synchronized. The statement of Galina Rikovskaya, my friend from the Cinema Institute, was typical of all the transcripts: "I will never believe that Luba was a spy. The only thing she ever told me about the Americans is that they were happy, friendly people and that she enjoyed attending picnics, concerts, and the theatre with them. But this isn't espionage."

Finally I agreed to give Vestov my signature verifying the evidence in the folder. As twisted as everything in Lubianka Prison was, Vestov, I discovered, had always recorded my replies during the interrogations with precision, and both my replies and the statements of my friends could only exonerate me from guilt.

10 IMPRISONMENT

Even though Vestov had never wavered from asserting my guilt, I could not now suppress a new surge of hope. At every interrogation session I had insisted on my innocence—and my friends had affirmed that fact. Vestov was one man and could make a mistake, I reasoned. But Vestov had informed me that my case would be judged by a *troika*, a court consisting of three men. Surely three men could not misread the evidence, I tried to convince myself as I sat hour after hour ramrod straight on my cell stool. My imprisonment was a misunderstanding—a tragic mistake. Now submitted to the *troika*, at last the error would be rectified.

Three days after my last interview with Vestov, one of the guards who had not spoken to me for nine months unlatched my cell door and announced with a scowl, "Collect your belongings. You are leaving." Leaving! However begrudgingly the guard had uttered the magic word, the wand had been waved. The *troika*, I told myself, had found me innocent.

Wreathed in smiles, I was escorted by the guard to the prison door I had entered nine months before. In the courtyard the guard prodded me into a raven-black prisoner transport van—marked with the word "bread" to disguise its true purpose—and locked me into a wire compartment. Even this stark setting did not sink my soaring spirits. Why should I care how they transported me. What mattered was that at last I was going home!

Mercifully my release had occurred so quickly that I had not had time to dwell on my homecoming. Now, however, I reached to straighten my stringy, oily hair and panic swept over me. Zhan must not see me like this. But he wouldn't be home at this hour. I would wash and dress before I would permit Dunya to call Zhan or Momma.

Through my reveries the van bumped to a halt and instantly a guard was opening the door, leading me out of the van into a courtyard circled with soldiers and growling German shepherd dogs. "Where am I?" I cried, again the child in the grasp of goblins. The guard who had opened the van door announced smugly, "You are in Butierka Prison."

"Prison!" I screamed.

"Silence!" Another guard beside me nudged me forward with his rifle, and suddenly I felt myself sinking in a quagmire of truth. I was again in prison. But no, I must not permit myself to perish in this morass of pessimism. Desperately I pulled my thoughts together. Vestov had released me from the Lubianka. If I was in prison again, it must be temporary. Perhaps, I desperately tried to convince myself, this place was a discharge point for prisoners about to be released.

Inside Butierka Prison, a guard shoved me into a cell the size of my bedroom on Sadovaya Street and which, stepping from the isolation of Lubianka Prison, seemed to me to be occupied by a crowd. In reality, there were twenty-eight women, all political prisoners like me, in the Butierka cell.

"Where did you come from? Do you have any news of the outside? What are you charged with?" The women surrounded me, and when I discovered that Butierka was not a silent prison, for the first time in nine months I talked ceaselessly. I told the women about my interrogations and even managed a smile when I recounted Vestov's attempt to use Zhan's rabbit sketches as evidence against me. I described the transcriptions Vestov had shown me of the interviews with my friends. "So you see, the *troika* must vindicate me. I hope to be home by tomorrow," I declared.

The next morning at nine o'clock, a guard summoned me from the cell. I picked up the matted fox fur coat I had worn when I entered the Lubianka nine months before. "I'm going home, ladies! I'm going home," I announced to my new friends as I left them.

"Your verdict, Bershadskaya," the MGB officer came abruptly to the point when I had been ushered into an interrogation room. He handed me a paper. I seized it, expecting to read my release.

Instead, the lines blurring before my eyes, I saw that I had been sentenced to three years of prison under article 58–1A of the penal code: "The accused committed no crime, but in this particular instance could have committed one," the verdict stated. Below the indictment, the *troika* had added another paragraph, "Prisoner Bershadskaya refuses to confess her crime," the statement said. "She is stubborn, pro-American, and anti-Soviet."

Stumbling into the cell, my first concern was to suppress my tears. What a fool I had been before the women last night! Now my performer's pride made me resolve not to appear weak before them. But I had underestimated my sister prisoners. I was caught by the embraces of the women and comforted by their tears.

In the month I spent in Butierka, it was the support of those twenty-eight women, all of them professionals, educated and innocent like me, which saved my sanity. Now with the *troika's* verdict, I could no longer cling to the thread of hope that the MGB's terrible mistake in arresting me would be unraveled. For the first time I was left with nothing with which to construct reality but merciless, unreasonable facts.

In Lubianka Prison my own misery had been my only reference point. In Butierka Prison I heard from the other prisoners accounts of cruelty and betrayal which helped provide me some perspective on my own problems. I discovered that my arrest, which I had considered an exception, was a fate shared by thousands of so-called political prisoners, innocent victims of Stalin's paranoiac purges.

One of my cellmates, Mariya Kuzmina, an accountant in a government office, had lived in Moscow in a two-room apartment. One day Mariya's distant relatives, Nonna Ivanovna and her fifteen-year-old son Igor, appeared at Mariya's door. Nonna and her son greedily ate the bread and tea Mariya set before them and told their tragic story. Nonna's husband had abandoned her soon after Igor was born. During the war, Nonna had worked on a collective farm and had managed to grow enough food on her private patch of garden to prevent starvation. Now hungry, lice-infested, and exhausted, Nonna and Igor had arrived at Mariya's doorstep with nowhere else in the world to go.

"You have to help people in difficult moments. You can't turn them out into the street," Maryia explained, describing how she had given the largest, brightest room in her apartment to Nonna Ivanovna and her son and then pawned some furniture to buy food for her destitute relatives.

In the midst of these ministrations, Mariya was arrested. When summoned to sign the dossier of evidence collected against her, Mariya saw that the chief documents accusing her of anti-Soviet activities had been provided to the MGB by Nonna Ivanovna and Igor.

In Butierka Prison, I also met Esther Kogan, a sixty-year-old Jewess who had worked as the assistant of Grigory Ilich Kryuchkov, the noted Soviet political scientist. Esther had been arrested when she refused to join the Party. Always when Esther saw me crying she would try to comfort me. "Maybe we are the lucky ones, Luba Leontievna. Maybe prison is more sane than the madhouse outside these walls. But this insanity can't continue forever. The world won't forget us. The West will not be indifferent!" Often Esther, as heroic as her biblical namesake, would solace me with the assurance that "everybody who is arrested becomes part of God's chosen people."

The irony of Esther's expression, "chosen people," haunted me every time the warden scraped open our prison door with a fresh batch of orders in his hand and clangorously called out the names of those who had been selected for shipment from Butierka, only a transit prison, to more permanent strongholds in Siberia.

On December 13, 1946, I was summoned, almost a month after I had entered Butierka, still clutching my certainty of release. That freezing December morning I was the only prisoner corraled from our cell for transport. Once again I was loaded onto a raven-black prisoner van and at the railroad station herded into one of many lines of prisoners waiting to board a train. The train—destined for none of us knew where—snaked along the tracks, every section bloated with prisoners, all petty criminals and all men, except for five other women prisoners and me.

The same guard who had escorted me from Butierka Prison now ordered me onto the train. "All aboard! Hurry up now!" another guard standing at the train steps cried as cheerily as if he were welcoming passengers to an excursion to Leningrad. Inside the train a third guard prodded us six women down the train's corridor past passenger compartments intended for six people which were now each bursting with thirty men. "Faster! Faster, you cows!" the guard snarled, shoving us women into the concierge's tiny compartment at the end of the corridor.

Compared to the men's cells which we had just passed, our cage with a bench for four and space on the floor for two to sit was nearly spacious. "Thank God, at least we've a wall between us and the criminals," Lila, a Ukrainian peasant woman who was one of my cellmates, muttered.

"But they're harmless. They are only embezzlers and petty thieves. It's the real criminals, the rapists and murderers, who are dangerous," Luda, a political prisoner embarking on a second sentence and already a veteran of the Gulag, Stalin's chain of prison camps stretched across Siberia, informed the rest of us novices.

One of the women in our compartment, Olya, had been a convinced Communist on her way to becoming a Party member. I tried to believe that it was because arrest had so violently shattered her ideals that her language was so profane. While the other five of us mostly tried to shut out our misery with silence, sleep, and tears, Olya groaned and cursed so incessantly that by the third day I found myself suffocating, as much from her words as from the stale, foul air of the train.

"I beg you, Olya. Please stop swearing!" I exclaimed one day.

At first Olya stared at me as if my request were too outlandish to warrant an answer. Finally she said, "You're a child, Luba Leontievna. When you've been through hell, you will talk just like me."

"I'll never talk like you," I vowed to myself. As the train crawled so clumsily that our thin, cold bodies were bruised from the jolts, I wrapped my fox fur coat, now fetid with the odors of prison, around me and tried to find from it some fragrance of my past and its purity. I was a child. Momma and I were sitting before the fireplace of our Kiev apartment. Momma had been reading *Eugene Onegin,* while Dunya and I drank tea and ate butter rolls. As usual, loath to let an opportunity for instruction pass, Momma had reminded me, "Pushkin's Tatiana was a real lady, Lubasha. And that is what you will be. It is not circumstances which define a lady. It is her character, and that is something no one can ever take from you."

Twice each day a guard shoved salted fish and a wedge of bread for each of us through the bars of our compartment. The more sane among us knew we could not afford to eat the salted fish regularly without water, a mercy which was to be refused by the guards, except for three times, on our twenty-eight-day trip.

One night, midway in our journey, a young guard who often

stood silent sentry by our cell door suddenly spoke to us through the iron bars which had replaced the top section of the compartment door on this specially equipped prisoner train.

"Wake up, girls!" the guard whispered, opening our door and pushing a pail into our cell.

"It's hot soup! There was some left from the officers' dinner," he said sympathetically. "Eat it quickly! I have to return the pail before they miss it."

But our hunger and thirst could not be so swiftly slaked. For several seconds we all sat stupefied, staring at the pail. Finally the smell, the warm familiar aroma of boiled potatoes, startled me into action. "Quick! Does anybody have a spoon?" I asked. The soldier had risked his freedom to bring us the soup. We could not also ask him to find a spoon. The Ukrainian Lila pulled a large spoon without a handle from her satchel and passed it to me. But I would not be first. I handed the spoon to Olya, seated closest to me and also the thinnest of us all. She stared at the soup and started to cry.

"Hurry, girls! Hurry!" the guard was hissing through the bars.

Olya, as if she were pushing a boulder, shoved the pail toward Luda. But sturdy Luda insisted she should be last. She handed the spoon to Maria, a Latvian girl so weak from hunger that she slept day and night. "Quick, Masha!" Luda ordered. "You need this worse than any of us." Masha turned from the pail and curled back on the floor to sleep, the broken spoon in her hand.

I snatched the spoon from Masha, but at that moment the guard entered our cell. "They're coming!" he whispered and yanked the pail from us. "It's full!" he cried, lifting the pail. "You fools! You're crazy!"

Even Masha awoke at the commotion and when we comprehended that the soup pail with its tantalizing, transfixing aroma was gone, all six of us wept inconsolably.

Periodically during the twenty-eight day trip our sluggish train would stop to disgorge prisoners who died along the way. These corpses were stacked by the guards on trailers at the rear of the train. How I dreaded the thud of dead bodies being pulled along the corridor, a sound so unlike the footfall of any living person.

Hundreds of prisoners, we knew, were dying from cold, hunger, and thirst. During my last days in Butierka Prison, my mother had managed through a sympathetic guard to send a package to me.

The package had contained five oranges, and after my Butierka cellmates and I had eaten the first, I had hoarded the peelings in the pocket of my fur coat. Now on the train I shared these peelings with the women in my compartment, and it was the microscopic drops of liquid from those peelings which we credited with saving our lives.

New Year's Eve, Russia's most festive winter holiday, fell on the nineteenth day of our trip. It was my turn that night to sit on the floor snuggled for warmth next to Olya whose curses, which had grown weaker with hunger, now mingled with all our moans for water. That midnight a cry rang through the corridors of our car, "*S Novym Godom*—Happy New Year!" I roused myself from my misery to voice the traditional New Year's greeting and with tears recalled how Zhan and I had unfailingly exchanged that greeting with a kiss every year at the stroke of midnight.

On January 9, 1947, twenty-eight days after we had left Moscow, our train halted in Marinsk in Western Siberia. We six women were the last to leave the train. Weak from starvation and thirst, we stumbled from the train into the blinding white landscape and intoxicating winter air. As soon as we stepped from the train Masha collapsed on the ground beside me. Before I could lift her to her feet, a group of guards and growling German shepherd dogs surrounded us and started to drag her away. "She's alive! She's alive!" I screamed, slapping Masha's face and pulling her to stand like a tottering pole beside me. The guards shoved us toward the four other women from our compartment, and together our pathetic column managed to pull Masha along.

"Faster! No stopping!" the guards shouted, prodding us to hurry as we approached the last car of the train. Linked to the last car was a chain of trailers, the morgue for all the prisoners who had died during the trip. Although the guards marched between us and the trailers, under the canvases covering each trailer we caught grisly glimpses of corpses stacked like lumber.

The only way I could keep from collapsing was to concentrate on counting the trailers layered with corpses—one, two, three, four . . . eight. I could not count the bodies, but I could count the cars and somehow I promised myself I would write a eulogy for those eight carloads of dead prisoners to whom Masha minutes before had nearly been added.

From Marinsk Station, the five hundred of us prisoners who had survived the nightmare train trip slogged through the snow five miles to Marinsk Prison, our only escort the wrathful guards and their ferocious dogs. Surprisingly, it was when we entered the prison gates of Marinsk that we for the first time in weeks felt ourselves in a world of humans. Inside the Marinsk Prison gate, two columns of prisoners formed a path into the courtyard. These prisoners, kempt and healthy compared to us, each held a morsel of bread, candy, or salami, hoarded from a parcel from home, to greet us new prisoners— their own miserable memories of their entry into Marinsk etched in their minds.

But the guards would not permit us to fraternize. "Hurry! March! Into the showers, you filthy enemies," the guards bellowed, herding us six women into a large room with showers on every wall.

A woman guard shoved us into an assembly line. "The prisoner behind scrubs the back and washes the hair of the prisoner in front," she instructed. "Prisoners are permitted a maximum of three minutes directly under the shower!"

"Three minutes to wash away the filth of prison," I muttered to myself, nestling into the first spray of warm water I had felt since I had left Butierka Prison.

After the guard had outfitted us with black prison uniforms which were all the same size, we were marched to another room. An old man with a full beard, wearing a black prison uniform, greeted us civilly. "I am a doctor. I will examine and admit you." Fortunately the doctor had permission to speak to us privately to inquire about our health, and during my examinations he discovered that I was a ballerina from Moscow.

"I wish Prisoner Bershadskaya to come to my office," the doctor announced when the examinations were completed. The doctor's office also served as his living quarters. When I entered the room, I discovered ten other political prisoners, also from Moscow, seated around a table covered with bread, salami, cheese, cakes, and a feast such as I had not seen in nearly a year.

"But I forgot! You are half starved," the doctor exclaimed, swooping the food off the table and away from me. With apologies for his lack of hospitality, the doctor told me about a famous soccer player from Kiev whom he had treated only a few months before. The day after his convoy arrived in Marinsk, the athlete had been assigned to work in the prison hospital. His first assignment was to serve food to all the patients. Overwhelmed with hunger, the athlete ate sixty small fish cakes intended for the patients. "He died," the doctor explained, handing me a small chunk of bread. "I have seen more than one prisoner on the verge of starvation stuff himself when he finally found some food, only to die from his short-lived pleasure."

That evening the doctor escorted me to my barracks after he and his guests, starved for news of Moscow, had eked from me every drop of my stale news, which nevertheless was more recent than theirs. The doctor was apologetic as he brought me to the barracks door. "I am sorry, Luba Leontievna," he whispered. "I would like to invite you again to our soiree, but I don't know if I will be able to manufacture another excuse."

Inside the barracks, my five cellmates from the train clustered around me, alarmed that I, the healthiest of all, had been signaled out to accompany the doctor. "No, he's a good man," I reassured them. Wishing myself back in the doctor's office, I surveyed the barracks, not knowing that the room where I now stood, populated by three hundred women and furnished only with wooden planks, wooden slop buckets, and two small stoves, would be my home for the next three years.

One night shortly after I had arrived in Marinsk, I huddled with the other prisoners in our barracks around one of the two stoves. As we sat, ringed like rag piles around the room, a grumbling guard summoned two prisoners close to the door to help him with "an old lady that looks like a gunnysack."

The two prisoners returned to our barracks with an old woman as thin as a piece of cloth. But beaming from the face of this pathetic body was the most luminous smile I had ever seen. All of us prisoners surrounded the newcomer and were soon smothering her with questions. "*Babushka,* where have you come from? How could they arrest you . . . You are so old . . . Are you ill?"

"I'm ninety." A surprisingly strong voice spoke from the feeble body. "I am only here overnight. They are sending me on to another prison. They arrested me because I was preaching the gospel, and now they are taking me from prison to prison, from camp to camp. My Savior wanted this. My place is here among the wretched, and my mission is to tell everyone about our compassionate God who comforts those who suffer."

I had begun to weep as the woman spoke, and she now turned toward me. "Don't cry little one," she said with a smile. "Believe me that I am happy."

That night the old woman waved aside our concerns for her health and with a strength it seemed impossible such a feeble body could possess, stayed awake almost the entire night speaking to us about God. I, more knowledgeable about Christianity than most of the women in our barracks, had never heard anyone speak so familiarly of Christ. "Saint Paul tells us we must fill up the cup of Christ's suffering with our suffering," the *babushka* said. "I beg you to believe that Christ will come to you and walk with you through your sufferings and lead you to his kingdom."

11 RACHEL WEEPING

The next morning, as the old woman had predicted, she was summoned from the barracks and sent on, her few hours like an angel visitation to our hell-hole barracks. Her appearance had been so ephemeral as to seem almost unreal. Her words, however, remained, and I stored every one in my mind to bring out and cherish as I had done when a child with the treasures in my mother's trunks. Repeatedly the *babushka* had spoken about joy. Humanly speaking, there had never seemed a less suitable word to describe Marinsk Prison. Was it possible, as the *babushka* insisted, that there was another world where that word had not lost all meaning?

During the winter of 1947, food shortages and even famine once again swept across Russia. If food was scarce outside the prison, inside it became nearly as terrible as the fare on the transport train had been. By February, for most of Marinsk's fifteen hundred inmates there was no bread—only a broth made from turnips and rotten fish. "Bread! Bread!" Ironically, the same cries which had once sparked the Bolshevik Revolution now filled the camp.

By March the cart that brought our morning soup was followed by another collecting the corpses of prisoners who had died during the night—sometimes as many as seventy in the entire camp and, during the worst days, as many as twenty women from my barracks alone.

Prisoners half-crazed by starvation screamed at the ghoulish guards who had come to collect the dead prisoners. "You murderers! You swine! Even an animal doesn't kill its own kind." One stout guard dressed in a sheepskin *dushegreiki* vest and overcoat always retorted, "So what if you enemies starve. We can't afford to waste bullets on you."

It was night, the black hours when the death's sword usually struck the starving, that I dreaded most. Even the prisoners like me, who were not starving, could not escape at night the other, worse torture of Marinsk—60 to 70 degrees below zero weather and icy winds howling through the cracked windows of our barracks, which was not heated by its two wood-burning stoves during the night. On the coldest nights, we dared not sleep but, swathed in the blankets from our beds, forced ourselves to pace the floor to keep from freezing. How I longed for my fur coat, my comfort on freezing nights on the transport train, but it had been confiscated the first day at Marinsk when our prison uniforms were issued.

During my first months at Marinsk, I spent most days, as well as nights, inside the barracks. Like most of the prisoners at Marinsk, a transit prison, I was not assigned regular work. Occasionally, however, I was summoned to record data for new prisoners entering the camp. Another prisoner, a man about fifty years old, often worked with me at this job. One day we began to converse. "I've been in prison for ten years now," he said as remotely as if that terrible statistic had nothing to do with him. "I'm of the Yezhov vintage."

"Yezhov," I mumbled, recalling Stalin's evil henchman who had been the head of the MGB before Beria. "Thank goodness he's gone!"

"Don't show your political ignorance, Luba Leontievna," the man said wearily. "It's not just Yezhov, or even Stalin for that matter. It's the whole rotten system," he whispered.

In contrast to my nine solitary months in Lubianka, there were plenty of people with whom I could converse in Marinsk. But what energy did starving, freezing prisoners have for conversation? Therefore, during my first weeks at Marinsk, I too lapsed into silence and concentrated all my strength on survival.

And I was surviving—with greater stamina than most of the women around me. I closed my eyes and saw Zakharov. I was eight years old and out of breath from a strenuous set of exercises at the bar. Zakharov's baton was instantly prodding me back into action. "Ballerinas don't rest. Endurance! Strength! Stamina! That's what it takes to be a ballerina." Now, in prison, I found myself thankful for the rigorous regimen of ballet.

I was also thankful for all the years I had endured the discipline of the severe diet required of a ballerina. I, the privileged ballerina, was accustomed to hunger—to the necessity of always eating far less than I wished, to preserve my figure. Now the ceaseless gnawing hunger of Marinsk did not obsess me as it did other prisoners, who clutched and clawed for every morsel of food.

The most pitiful prisoners in my barracks were the old women, shrunken, shriveled, and often huddled together like wisps of straw in a haystack. As I watched the old women I constantly thought of my mother. How easily the insane Soviet system, which snared prisoners like a butterfly chaser with a net, might have captured her. What if she were one of those thin, shivering bodies crouched around the iron stove?

Perhaps it was my great gratitude that my mother had been spared from prison which in some mysterious way opened a window to me and began to shed small sustaining slants of light on my own prison experience. I was strong. I could survive. I *would* survive. But somehow I must help the weaker ones.

I recalled one Sunday when I was five years old and my mother had stopped as usual at the French bakery after church. It was the week before Easter, and the *bulochki* were decorated with white icing in the shape of a cross and smothered with raisins. My mother bought two dozen *bulochki*, and I was not surprised when she stopped to give one dozen buns to the poor Vechikov family with six children who lived near the church. But when my mother handed nine more of the remaining buns to Mrs. Vechikov, I had sulked. My mother did not scold me but gently said, "We are fortunate and rich and strong, Lubasha. All these gifts are for sharing with the unfortunate and weak. Stingy people hoard their happiness and then they become unhappy."

Compared to many of the miserable, sick, starving souls around me at Marinsk, I was still, I knew, the fortunate, strong one. But how could even a drop of happiness be shared in this place where most people were too wretched to speak or, if they did, only babbled crazily like Lila Nahumovich, a sixty-nine-year old woman who was the daughter of a czarist army general and mother of a Soviet army colonel?

As hopeless as Lila's situation seemed, I decided to speak to her and try to comfort her. On rare days she replied normally, describing to me her life as a piano teacher and French teacher. On other days she sat in a corner and crooned French love songs, sometimes dancing in a slow, swaying rhythm to the accompaniment of her own songs.

One day two guards pulled Lila, screaming and kicking, from our barracks to the shower room. A guard scrubbed her thin skin until it turned red and handed her clean clothes and new boots. "You're going to be released. Your son is coming to take you home today," the woman guard announced. But when Lila was escorted to her colonel son, she did not recognize him and pled to be permitted to return to the barracks.

Anya, a woman my age and a loyal, devoted Communist, was another of the prisoners I tried to cheer. Anya, who lived in Moscow, had gone to visit her mother in Minsk. While in Minsk she decided to take some photos to commemorate her visit and found the perfect place to pose for the photos—a life-size statue of Lenin seated on a stone bench. Anya and her mother stood beside the statue while a friend snapped their photo. To pose for the next photo, Anya sat on Lenin's lap. For that sacrilege she had been arrested.

Now in Marinsk, Anya arose every morning and lifted the board which served as the mattress on her plank bed. On the board Anya had written, "I am Lenin's daughter." Every morning, as regularly as the gong that awakened us, Anya plodded barefoot with the board across the snow to the officers' hut and stationed herself in front of the building. Every morning guards came and pulled her shrieking through the snow back to our barracks.

"If only Lenin were alive, he would understand," Anya would frequently moan after her morning vigil. "Why don't you write to Stalin?" someone suggested to Anya.

When I was a child, Dunya had told me how petitioners in czarist days approached their mighty ruler. Of course it was unthinkable, Dunya had explained, for common citizens to directly approach Russia's exalted czar, the "Little Father." But sometimes peasants would write a request on a piece of paper and tape this petition to their foreheads to attract the czar's attention when he was passing by in a procession.

Now Stalin was Russia's "Little Father," a title still used by millions of Russians, including many Marinsk prisoners who could not bring themselves to ascribe their misfortune to the man they had believed to be Russia's savior. To disabuse the ignorance of these prisoners who still considered Stalin their most faithful friend seemed to me a cruelty. The kindest course, I decided, was to help the prisoners, often illiterate peasants, compose letters to Stalin. Thus in Marinsk I began my career as Luba the letter writer, composing hundreds of letters to Stalin during both my prison terms.

Antonia Dmitrievna, a simple, hardy Ukrainian woman in her sixties, was one of the many prisoners for whom I composed letters. Antonia had lived on a collective farm near Kharkov, but owned a small private plot of land. Besides the plot, Antonia's most prized possessions in the world were two young goats. Antonia, a Soviet patriot, decided to bestow the highest honor she could imagine on the goats. She named one Lenin and the other Stalin.

Every morning Antonia summoned the goats from the back door of her cottage. "Here, Lenin! Here, Stalin! Where have you gone to now, you stupid little Stalin?" she would cluck affectionately to the kid inclined to stray the farthest.

Unfortunately a neighbor overheard Anya's endearments and raced with his accusation to the MGB. Now, five years later, in Marinsk, Anya told me her story, still as mystified by her plight as she had been from the first day of her arrest when she was charged with anti-Soviet slander. But it had not occurred to Anya to blame Stalin, and she eagerly seized my offer to help her write a letter to her hero. "Dear Comrade Stalin," Anya dictated, "please believe me when I tell you I am innocent. Please forgive me, Father Stalin, if I have offended you in some way I do not know. You are our kindest and best leader. I plead with you to let me return to my family."

I, like all Marinsk prisoners, longed for a letter from all my family, and some days the lack of a letter seemed a harsher deprivation than scarce food. I, according to the rules of my prison sentence, was not permitted any correspondence privileges at Marinsk. I was, however, permitted one package per year from my family, and my first package arrived in the winter of 1948, filled with garlic, onions, butter, sausage, and bread. Near the bottom of the package lay two pounds of sugar in a bright green cloth sack. I emptied the sugar into a bottle and, thankful for the patch of color, folded the green cloth at the foot of my bed. Two *babushkas* stood beside me, stroking the green cloth. "It's for you, sisters," I said suddenly, swooping the cloth from my bed to their hands.

By now, other women were circling my bed, watching as I unwrapped my parcel. I handed out the onions and garlic, so necessary for combatting scurvy. I broke the sausage in chunks and distributed that too. At the very bottom of my parcel, I discovered a white paper with a child's sketch of a large wooden *dacha* and green trees. "Love to Momma from Vladislav," large slanting letters at the bottom of the page said. I turned from the women clustered around my parcel and crouched alone in a corner with the precious message, careful that my tears should not blot Vladik's painting.

I was not the only prisoner to be stricken by a communication from a child. I thought of the story I had heard of a woman who had been imprisoned when her son was two years old. For ten years she had heard nothing from her family, and it was not until her son was twelve that they managed to find her and send a parcel. In the package was a photo of a group of young boys. On the back of the picture the woman's son had written, "Momma, guess where I am in the photo?" The distraught woman, unable to recognize her son, died that night from a heart attack.

In March, a month after the package from home had helped break the bleakness of my first winter at Marinsk, another event buried the entire camp in mourning.

One bitter, black morning I was summoned to help process a contingent of new prisoners. "Hurry! There are a lot of them," a female guard commanded, her voice strangely subdued compared to the usual cranky tone that characterized her orders. When I reached the room where prisoners were processed, I understood why even our calloused guard, perhaps a mother herself, seemed softened. Three hundred and twenty women, clutching to their breasts emaciated babies mostly too weak to whimper, sat ringed around the room, waiting.

The women, I learned, had all been pregnant at the time of their arrests and had given birth in prisons all over the Soviet Union. The MGB had gathered them together with their infant children into one prison in Moscow. There the authorities had told the mothers, "You are going to be sent on to the other prisons. You will leave your children with us, and the government will see that they are reared properly."

The mothers had moaned, screamed, shaken their fists, and refused this order with such violence that the authorities had seemingly relented and given approval for the babies to accompany their mothers to Siberia.

"But how did your baby survive the train trip?" I could not stop weeping as I sat beside a woman suckling a child on a withered breast that seemed to offer no nourishment. The woman, her eyes haunted and her body haggard, began to weep too. "They wanted to tear Oleg away from me," she kept repeating. "I'll die first," she murmured, stroking the limp, little body that lay at her breast.

I longed to stop and cuddle each child—a tiny prisoner wrapped in rags, staring with adult eyes. But the officials kept hurrying them and shouting to the mothers, "Wrap your children as warmly as you can. We are taking you all to a better place."

"Couldn't they at least wait for warmer weather?" I grumbled to another prisoner.

"Any place would have to be better than this hell," my co-worker replied.

Finally, a prison guard ordered the mothers with their babies outdoors. "March in formation!" he shouted. "The wagons are waiting for you at the prison gate." I trailed after this pitiful contingent, handing my jacket to a mother beside me whose baby shook with cold.

"Babies on the wagons. Mothers will walk behind!" shouted the same guard when the mothers reached the wagons. "Place your babies in the straw." The guard formed a megaphone with his hands as he stood atop the first of the six wagons lined in formation to pass through the one narrow prison gate.

It was while the head guard was issuing these orders that I noticed rows of male guards forming behind the mothers. Was it curiosity, I wondered, that brought them to watch this sad spectacle? Could it possibly be compassion?

As tenderly as if they were swaddling their children in silk blankets, the mothers placed the babies in the straw heaped atop each wagon, creating a garden of nativity scenes. "Hurry!" the head guard called from atop the first wagon. The fifty babies tucked in the straw at his feet whimpered and mewed as their mothers turned from them. "The faster we load, the sooner we will arrive at the next camp," the guard said. "The wagons with babies will drive through the gate first," he instructed. "Mothers will walk, following twenty paces behind the wagons."

The mothers hung back obediently, their arms empty, clinging to each other for strength. "Go!" the guard shouted and in synchronization the six wagons started to move, the clopping of the horses' hooves sounding through the wails of the frightened babies. Slowly, steadily, the horses plodded through the narrow gates.

The woman to whom I had given the jacket handed it back to me, her eyes on the wagon ahead, her body trembling to follow. The last wagon passed through the prison gate. I embraced the woman for a second and shoved her toward the gate. "Go! Go! Now you can follow your baby!"

But at that instant, when the last wagon wheel had rolled through the gate, guards on either side of the gateposts leaped outside and swung shut the iron gates. For a second the mothers could not grasp the horror of what was happening, but then they were surging toward the gates, clawing at the iron bars, thrashing at the guards who were pinioning their arms and pulling them away.

Like Rachel weeping for her children, the mothers were dragged away from the gate to a barracks isolated from the rest of the camp, and I was never permitted to mingle with them again. But the wrenching agony of that scene would remain with me forever, a memory like the trailer of corpses from the transport train, coming to me in nightmares and haunting me during the day when I had to reckon with the reality that this torment had really happened. And who in the world would ever know or care about the three hundred and twenty mothers and their babies? Like the corpses from the train, their story too would be buried in Siberian snows.

"I won't let that happen. I will never allow them to be forgotten," one voice inside me promised. But another voice always taunted, "Who are you? Who will believe you? Maybe you yourself will die in prison." After the incident with the mothers, I would often awake at night shouting and flailing my arms from the same recurring nightmare. The mothers were standing wailing before the closed prison gate and I was trying to push them through.

I thought there could be no more tragic prisoners in Marinsk or in all the world than the three hundred and twenty mothers. But in 1947, with Christmas approaching, I discovered another group of Marinsk prisoners whose plight was nearly as pathetic.

That December a blizzard pounded Marinsk, making our ramshackle flimsy barracks more miserable than ever. Now besides the cold, the wind blasted frozen snow through the cracks in our barracks.

One night, so cold I feared I might freeze to death if I lay still and slept, I paced the barracks floor and in my circuits passed a woman weeping hysterically who was trying to muffle her sounds with a pillow. I stopped to comfort her and realized it was Valya Andreyevna, a nurse from the city of Kishniev who was seldom in the barracks during the day, usually away on medical tasks assigned by the authorities.

"It's the thirty women in the seventh barracks," Valya sobbed. "I can't stand it any longer." I circled Valya's shoulders with my arm and asked her to tell me about the women. "They're believers," she said. "The MGB arrested them after the war and accused them of praying for the Germans. Now they won't eat; they won't even put on clothes. The authorities force me to go every day to feed them with liquids by enema." Valya started to shudder. "I can't go back. I can't stand to see them suffer," she sobbed.

"Valya," I whispered, "I want to see them. Let's go right now," I said, taking her prison jacket from beside her bed.

"But the night watchman," Valya worried. "What if he sees us?"

"We'll be careful. We won't be discovered," I reassured her, although I had no certainty we would not be stopped.

It was the stench—the sour odor of unwashed, sickly bodies— that first met us as we entered the dimly lit barracks. Then it was the sight, so inhuman I swayed against the barracks wall. Stretched before us were rows of naked bodies, the grizzled, ghoulish tormented creatures of Michaelangelo's *Last Judgment*.

In one corner of the barracks stood a stack of blankets and prison uniforms. "Why are they naked?" I whispered to Valya.

"Sister Anya? Sister Anya?" A voice from one of the naked bodies quavered through the darkness.

"Sister Anya is their leader. They won't dress and they won't eat until she comes," Valya explained. "They say that only Sister Anya has power to tell them what to do. But none of us knows who Sister Anya is."

That night after Valya and I had returned to our barracks— which seemed almost comfortable after the misery I had seen—I continued to pace the floor. By the next morning I had formed a plan.

That night I borrowed Valya's white nurse's scarf and a long black Ukrainian skirt from another prisoner. "I hope Momma would forgive me for lying," I said to Valya, outlining my plan as we darted through the prison courtyard.

As soon as we stepped into the seventh barracks Valya announced in a stentorian voice, "I have brought Sister Anya to you!" I, with my kerchief tied like an Orthodox nun's, moved to the center of the room.

In the dim light the naked bodies clustered around me, clutching my hands, kneeling, praying, and exclaiming, "Sister Anya! Sister Anya!" A torrent of tears fell on my face, and I tried to calm myself while they prayed.

When I could speak I said, "My dear, dear sisters." At least every word I had said so far was truthful. But then I pressed on, not knowing what to say. "Before we start discussing our business," I said—not knowing what business I could fabricate to discuss—"I allow you, I beg you, to put on your clothing and tell the authorities that you will take food."

The women, with more energy than I had thought such husks of bodies could possess, scurried to the pile in the corner and began to put on the clothing. "Nurse Valya and I will help you make your beds," I offered, reaching for the blankets.

When the women had dressed and made their beds, they clustered around me with a rapt expression, waiting for my important announcement. Any story I would invent, I told myself, could not be more crushing than the truth of their atrocious situation. "Your case is under review in Moscow," I announced and then vaguely I spun a tale about courage for the present, since help must inevitably come in the future. "I must leave you again. For now, I want you to be brave and eat and dress and hold to your faith in God," I concluded.

With my mission accomplished, I did not intend to return to the seventh barracks, but contented myself with reports from Valya. The women had continued to eat and cooperate with the guards, she told me. But as Christmas approached and parcels from home cheered prisoners in my barracks, I could not put Sister Anya's nuns from my mind.

I still had a few onions and some garlic from a box Zhan and Momma had sent me. I put these in a box and carried the box from bunk to bunk. "For the poor ones who didn't receive any parcel," I said. "Please give something from yours."

On January 6, the eve of Russian Orthodox Christmas, Valya and I schemed once again to help the suffering women in the seventh barracks. Valya draped a black camp blanket around my shoulders, tied a borrowed red rag around my waist, and arranged another rag in a turban on my head. I was Grandfather Frost—not the plump, elegantly attired Grandfather Frosts who circled my childhood Christmas tree, but the red rag signaled clearly a genuine, if shabbier, version of the legendary Russian Christmas figure.

Once again Valya and I hurried through the courtyard to the seventh barracks. Valya flung open the barracks door and exclaimed, "Good evening, dear ladies. Grandfather Frost has come to you!" The nuns, now clothed but still caught in the trance that had characterized their motions the first time I met them, edged toward the table where I was emptying the contents of my box.

I, hoping none of them would notice my resemblance to Sister Anya, handed gifts to each of them, accompanying each presentation with the words, "I greet you with the Christ's birth!"

12 RELEASE

In 1947 the director of Marinsk Prison was transferred and a new commandant, Colonel Prokofiev, was dispatched from Moscow. The former director had never mingled with prisoners, but Prokofiev often walked through the prison grounds, and the amazing news filtered through the camp that he even addressed prisoners by their names—not "enemy!" or the other demeaning titles to which we were accustomed.

Besides administrating Marinsk, Colonel Prokofiev was also commandant for all camps in that *siblag* or administrative region of Siberia, of which Marinsk, with its fifteen hundred inmates, was the largest. One day Prokofiev announced that he had received a decree from Moscow authorizing him to organize talent performances utilizing the many prisoners in his *siblag* who had been actors, musicians, dancers, or any kind of artist in their former life. This "Theatre of the Serfs," as we prisoners came to call it, was primarily intended to entertain prison staff and citizens in the nearby town of Marinsk. When convenient, prisoners might also view the performances inside the camp.

The small town of Marinsk, three kilometers from Marinsk Prison, was populated primarily by prison guards, officers, and their families. A hospital located in the center of Marinsk for the prison staff was also used for prisoners from all the *siblag*. Next to the hospital stood a spacious, seldom-used Communist club, and Prokofiev decided that this building would be our theatre.

Our first gathering of prisoner performers was held, however, inside Marinsk Prison in an empty barracks which Prokofiev had designated as our rehearsal hall. Prokofiev stood on a stage which had been hastily constructed in the barracks and addressed about one hundred of us artists who waited as apprehensively as a child who fears its new toy might be snatched away.

But the incredible, according to Prokofiev, was true, authorized by the Kremlin itself. "You will primarily serve the citizens of Marinsk but occasionally perform before other prisoners also," Prokofiev explained. "You will receive additional allotments of food and clothing. You will be permitted to bathe twice every ten days instead of once. Supplies such as makeup and wigs have been ordered from Moscow," I heard Prokofiev say and fingered the stiff strands of my hair. Maybe for the first time since my fateful interview with Reikhman at the Lubianka, I might see my face in a mirror.

"You will not, I am sorry to say, be permitted to stage Soviet plays, only classics." Prokofiev's words broke through my reverie. "As political prisoners, it would be a sacrilege for you to present Soviet drama," Prokofiev announced sternly. Of course we did not dare even smirk at Prokofiev's words, but when we were alone we laughed and rejoiced at the Communist prohibition intended to be a punishment. To have been forced to perform obtuse Soviet patriotic plays with predictable plots had always been a bore to any of us who were true artists. Now, to mouth their obsequious dialogue lauding our captors would have been torture.

Prokofiev did not guess how he had spared us. Neither could even such a comparatively decent official as Prokofiev know the gift Moscow's decree was to us artists. Now every day we could meet with other artists, immerse ourselves in the rehearsals and performances, and temporarily escape from our wretched prison world.

After his speech Prokofiev permitted us artists to mingle with each other and with lightning speed we got acquainted. The first person I met was Gega Muria, a former star of the Estonian opera. Gega, imprisoned in another camp of the Marinsk *siblag* for seven years, had not seen soap all that time, and I promised myself the pleasure of bringing her a piece and watching the transformation of this ragged creature back to a beautiful opera singer. That day I also met Dolli Takeryan, a Hungarian dancer only thirty-five but so emaciated she looked sixty, as well as Nikoli Zhukov, a singer, and Ivan Turenkov, a composer from White Russia. We all exchanged introductions as courteously as if we were meeting for the first time at the Bolshoi. Besides the artists from the Soviet Union, there were several from Yugoslavia, Hungary, and Romania. "What an elegant, cosmopolitan group we are," I teased.

"You won't be laughing when we put on our wigs, Luba Leontievna," Nikolai Sergeyevich Khrobko, director of the Moscow television center, said, his cheeks so sunken that he seemed to struggle to find the strength for a smile. That day we chose Nikolai Sergeyevich to be our drama director. His assistant was Larissa Larskaya Petrova, an older actress who had performed in prerevolutionary theatres. I was appointed choreographer, and, to direct all artistic events, we chose Ivan Adamovich Raizin, a talented man who had been both a singer and director in the Tbilisi Theatre.

Nikolai Sergeyevich Khrobko immediately suggested a play for our first production—*The Stepmother* by Honore Balzac. By our second meeting, Nikolai Sergeyevich had assigned roles. Larissa Larskaya would be the stepmother and I the stepdaughter. Thus, my bizarre career as an actress and dancer in the "Theatre of the Serfs" began and lasted the remainder of my two years at Marinsk.

Almost every morning we rehearsed in the Marinsk barracks which had been set aside by Prokofiev for our rehearsal hall. Sometimes as frequently as twice a week we performed plays or presented dances and concerts at the theatre in Marinsk.

On the nights we performed in Marinsk, Prokofiev extended our curfew to twelve o'clock. Like Cinderella, reality came crashing through our lives at midnight. Wigs and finery removed, we lined up in ranks of five for the three-kilometer trek back to the prison camp, once again a convoy of prisoners snaking through the snow, surrounded by guards and snarling German shepherd dogs.

Ivan Adamaovich Raizin, our kindly artistic director, tried to enlist as many prisoners as possible in our ranks in order for them to benefit from the extra food rations and bonus showers permitted performers. "I can't operate a theatre without stagehands and lighting crew and makeup artists," Raizin insisted to prison authorities who scarcely understood our plays, much less what it took to produce them. But such deceptions had to be carried out with caution since one fixture of our prison world did not disappear even inside the theatre. Everywhere, even in the women's dressing room, sullen guards surrounded us like pillars.

Each evening inside the prison camp, two guards delivered extra bread to our rehearsal hall. We performers took turns cutting the loaves into sixty-gram portions which would be distributed next morning at rehearsal. One Tuesday night, after a performance in Marinsk, I sliced the bread and weighed each portion on a scale, entertaining myself as I did so by memorizing the lines for the new play we were producing—*The Hunchback of Notre Dame*.

Suddenly through the barred window beside me I heard scraping sounds. I had heard stories of guards and demented prisoners attacking women they found alone. I would be safer where my screams could be heard, I decided, striding out of the empty room.

Outside, I discovered a man pacing below my window and in the light from the guard tower I recognized the form of our drama director, Nikolai Sergeyevich Khrobko.

"Luba, don't be frightened. It is I," he whispered, turning toward me.

"But dear Nikolai Sergeyevich," I said, "why aren't you sleeping? Won't you come in?"

"I could smell the bread as I walked by," Nikolai Sergeyevich said sheepishly. "Perhaps it is difficult for you to cut so many loaves. May I help you?"

Instantly I understood. My aristocratic Nikolai Sergeyevich was hungry, so hungry he could not resist the aroma of the bread, and his good manners would not permit him to ask me for a piece.

"My dear guest, sit down," I said, finding him a chair and playing the role of hostess with all the courtesy my mother had instilled in my childhood games in Kiev. "It just happens that tonight I have extra bread available," I said, chopping off my own portion and that of two others who I knew would not mind. I arranged the bread on a piece of paper which I folded like a plate and handed it to Nikolai Sergeyevich.

Ravenous as he was, Nikolai Sergeyevich did not begin to eat immediately, but seated me in my chair and settled himself in a proper manner at the table. "And you, Luba Leontievna"—his hand trembled as he held the bread toward me. "Won't you join me?"

"You know the breadcutter is never hungry," I replied with a wink. "I have already had my fill. But please don't wait, Nikolai Sergeyevich, your bread will get cold."

Gallant Nikolai Sergeyevich was so engrossed in his meal that he forgot to laugh, and I tried not to notice how his hand shook when he lifted the last crumbs from the paper to his lips.

Nikolai Sergeyevich had not stopped to speak while he ate, but now when I offered him a cup of limpid tea boiled from leaves left from the morning rehearsal, he leaned forward on his chair to converse. "You know, Luba, our audience in Marinsk has been in a fog all through *The Stepmother*. They will never understand Schiller's *Treachery in Love* when we begin our performances next month. What an imbalance between the content of these plays and the intellect of our audience!"

"What difference does it make, Nikolai Sergeyevich?" I said, laying my hand on his. "We will be our own audience, and thank God for all the hours when we can lose ourselves in the world of beauty and art and forget where we really are."

Uncomprehending as our Marinsk audience was, they applauded *The Stepmother* wildly and, as dutifully as serfs bowing to the wishes of their masters, we extended the play week after week with Larissa Larskaya playing the role of the jealous stepmother and I the victimized stepdaughter.

One evening before the final act of *The Stepmother*, Larissa whispered to me, "I don't feel well, Lubasha!" When the curtain fell after the last act, Larissa staggered from the stage.

"Maybe it is your corset. Here let me unloosen it!" I cried, thinking that the costume which made Larissa look at least twenty years younger must have been tied too tightly. But even before I could reach her, Larissa collapsed on the stage, dead from a heart attack.

That evening as our tearful convoy marched back from Marinsk to the prison camp, two guards pulled the body of Larissa Larskaya on a sled.

Early the next morning Nikolai Khrobko, Ivan Raizin, and a delegation of ten other of us performers knocked at Prokofiev's office.

"No doubt you have heard of the death of our colleague, Larissa Larskaya Petrova," Khrobko stated courteously to Prokofiev's assistant who received us. "We have come to ask permission to bury her."

The officer crushed the cigarette he had been smoking under

his boot. "Look what the enemies have come up with now," he sneered. "Next thing they will be wanting a priest."

"And why not?" Khrobko said softly.

"Don't forget where you are. You may be an artist, but here you are nothing but a prisoner, you fascist swine," the officer shouted, slapping Nikolai Sergeyevich in the face.

In an instant Ivan Raizin's fist shot toward the officer, pushing the man's head out from under his cap. Terrified, the rest of us flung ourselves at Ivan Adamovich and tried to pull him away.

"Ivan Adamovich," I panted, "it won't help. They'll throw you in solitary or worse!" Before I could say more, the guards had Ivan in a pillorylike grasp and were pulling him away from us.

For twelve days we heard nothing of Ivan Adamovich. "It is my fault. He was only trying to defend me." Nikolai Sergeyevich paced the planks of the rehearsal hall, wringing his hands, like the rest of us too distraught to concentrate on our work. Through the unofficial prison communications network we eventually learned that Prokofiev had tried to prevent Ivan Adamovich from being punished. But a new MGB official now occupied a position in the *siblag* that superseded Prokofiev, and Raizin was shipped to a strict regime prison.

All our pleas for the noble Larissa Larskaya were also in vain. She was buried with strict adherence to the rules of Marinsk Prison, a wooden tag with her prison number tied to her foot. None of us performers were permitted to be present when two guards tossed her into a hole which was soon covered by a Siberian snowstorm.

Each performance of the "Theatre of the Serfs," besides permitting slight rays of sunshine into our dark existence, also became for me a kind of calendar marking the days until my release. While I tried to distract myself with the "Theatre of the Serfs," the real drama of my life, I prayed, was moving inexorably toward freedom. Counting the time I had spent in Lubianka and Marinsk prisons, my three-year term was scheduled, I knew, to end March 20, 1949.

By January 1949 Marinsk Prison had not changed. At night there was still no heat in the barracks, and frigid air reached through rag-stuffed windows to torment the three hundred hungry, exhausted bodies who populated my barracks. But in a mysterious manner, only explicable by the fact that March 20 was less than three months away, the winter of 1949 somehow seemed to me more bearable. I had survived the worst trial of my life. Unlike so many of the other wounded women around me, I not only had my sanity but my integrity and even my health. After this trial, nothing worse in life could ever befall me, I told myself.

During the night of March 19 I paced our barracks floor, for once not driven by the cold as much as the tormenting uncertainty of the next day. "Calm yourself, Luba Leontievna, calm yourself." Sonya Semyonovna, an elderly woman whose feet were perpetually raw from the undersized prison boots that had been issued to her, hobbled toward me. "You'll wear yourself out with hopes and be too weak to walk away tomorrow." She, sentenced to a ten-year term herself, tried to console me.

"Take no thought for the morrow. That's what the Scriptures say," Sonya admonished. I gave her my arm and helped her toward a wooden bench. I preferred to be alone with my thoughts, but perhaps Sonya needed the comfort of consoling me. At least I would not force her to walk and add to her pain.

"Give me any advice you have, Sonya Semyonovna," I said, settling us both on the hard bench.

"It is just like eating too much after you have been starved. Too much excitement can kill you in the end. Take the case of Ivan Mikhailovich," Sonya said. "He was sent to prison for fifteen years and never allowed to receive a letter from his wife and son in the Ukraine during all that time. But then, one month before his release, he was permitted to write a letter home. His wife replied immediately and told him to wait at the prison until she came to meet him. But Ivan's wife was not able to reach his prison by the day of his release and Ivan, now a free man, refused to spend one night longer than necessary inside the camp. Since it was summer, he decided to sleep on the grass and wait for his wife to arrive. That night a terrible Siberian thunderstorm came and before poor Ivan Mikhailovich could run for shelter, he was struck and killed by a bolt of lightning." Sonya sighed.

After this less-than-comforting tale about Ivan, Sonya pulled other stories from her well-stocked larder of prison lore, and in this way my last night in prison passed more swiftly than if I had paced the floor alone.

"Prisoner Bershadskaya is summoned to the camp director. Report immediately after breakfast." A guard discharging the last duty of his night shift wearily read the morning announcements to our barracks. I did not dare go immediately to the director's office, but filed as usual with the other women to breakfast. As soon as our gruel breakfast was served, I shoved it toward the prisoner next to me. "Here, you can have it all. And my spoon—you can keep that too. I won't be needing it anymore," I said dashing toward the door to the director's office.

"It is the warmest day we have had yet. Perhaps spring is coming soon." An officer greeted me as courteously as if I were already a civilian. "This is your free ticket provided by the Soviet government to the destination where your term began," the officer said. Thank God, they were sending me all the way to Moscow, I thought. "This is your release document. Guard it with your life. It is the only authorization for the militia, the police station in Marinsk, to issue you a passport."

A passport! Then there was no doubt—no possibility I was walking in my sleep and might find myself shooed back to my barracks when I tried to walk away from Marinsk forever. As ignorant as I had been of most matters pertaining to the Soviet system before prison, even then I had known the importance of a passport. Housing, schooling, work, travel—everything for a Soviet citizen hinged on that one tiny document. The saying, "A person without a passport has no identity," was not an exaggeration.

Heedless of Sonya Semyonovna's cautions about haste, I fled from the director's office back to my barracks and in minutes had distributed my few treasures to those who remained behind. "The onions and garlic are for the *babushkas*," I said, handing out the remains of my last parcel from home. I handed my comb to Liza Dmitrievna, a pretty Ukrainian girl with long, golden hair.

Farewells to three hundred people were not as simple to distribute. Confident of my release, I had said good-bye to all my friends from the theatre after a performance two nights before. Now came the barracks farewells, mostly to women in transit whom I had not known long.

The farewell that will forever be etched in my memory occurred when I walked through the gates of Marinsk. Arrivals and departures

were common at Marinsk, and I had not wanted to create a commotion. It was better to leave quickly, not turn back, not linger over
futile feelings. On the morning of March 20, 1949, I walked through
Marinsk Prison gate alone for the first time in three years. But I was
not alone. Behind me I heard my name in a roar. Not prisoner, not
enemy, but Luba, Lubasha, Luba Leontievna. Behind me, circled
on top of the barracks which rose above Marinsk's barbed wire,
stood a thousand prisoners waving, calling, and wishing me good
luck in a torrent of affection I had never seen displayed for any
released prisoner.

But paradoxically their kindness did not free me. In a paroxysm
of guilt I suddenly felt myself more imprisoned than I had ever been
before. Walking backwards, I waved to my friends and for a tormented moment felt a tug to run back towards them. They were as
innocent as I. Why should I be leaving? I turned from them, unable
to bear the sight any longer and unable to see through the scalding
tears flowing down my face.

I stumbled down the road, dazed with sorrow and guilt. And
then, when I was out of sight of the camp, alone in a rime-covered
field, I heard myself screaming—terrifying, rending shrieks which
I could not silence.

Like a patient coming out of a coma, I finally pulled myself
to consciousness on the white field. Practical considerations pressed
on me. Marinsk was still three kilometers away. The train to Moscow, other prisoners had told me, departed in the early evening. I
still had to obtain my passport.

But my passport proved to be no problem—at least that was
what I thought when a clerk in the police office handed it to me in
ten minutes. However, another seemingly insurmountable obstacle
loomed before me. How could I notify my family that I had been
released? Had they possessed as much confidence as I that I would
actually be released after three years? And even if they had, how
would they know where to meet me? Strangely, after all I had survived during the last three years, the dread of returning to Moscow
unmet by my family hurt more painfully than Marinsk's miseries.

Deciding I would try to send my family a telegram, I ran to
the railroad station office. "*Pozhaluysta,* . . . please, sir," I said,
addressing the stationmaster with polite words I had scarcely had

occasion to utter in the camp. "Can you direct me to the telegraph office? I must tell my family I am coming home!"

"It is here in the station," the stationmaster replied. "But it is closed."

"Closed?" I repeated weakly, tears welling in my eyes.

"I will permit you to use the telephone in my office," the kindly stationmaster offered.

I called my home. No answer. I tried again and let it ring longer. Still no answer. Next I called my sister Ira. No answer. By the time I dialed Styopa and Maria's number and no one answered, my hands were trembling. A terrible presentiment seized me and I shook with fear. They have all been arrested. But Oh, God, not the children . . . and Momma, and Dunya.

The stationmaster regarded me with pity. "The train's coming soon, comrade," he said gently, taking my arm and guiding me toward the platform. "You wouldn't want to miss the train home, would you."

13 REARREST

Through the torture of my twenty-eight-day train trip to Marinsk in 1946, it had seemed to me that Marinsk must be at least 5,000 miles from Moscow. In reality, the distance was eight hundred miles covered by normal trains in twenty-six hours.

As normal as the train I now boarded on March 20, 1949 seemed in comparison to the cattle car in which I had ridden to Marinsk in 1946, I was not yet to be entirely regarded as a regular passenger. The ticket issued by the prison camp, I learned, guaranteed me a place in the train—not a seat. A conductor squeezing through the slitted aisles motioned me to a passageway by the window. "That's all we've got, comrade. Take it and be grateful you don't have to stand all the way to Moscow!"

And of course I was grateful, beyond even my own comprehension, to be free and homeward bound. Nevertheless, even as this wave of comfort rolled over me, another wave followed swiftly behind to push it away. I had received a few parcels, but for three years I had not been permitted to receive a single letter from my family. Did I still have a home?

Before the train had traveled many miles, suffocating heat flooded the compartments. I recalled our icy compartment on the prison train. "Can't they do anything in moderation?" I grumbled drowsily, discovering that too much heat was at least conducive to sleep. But that night, propped against the side wall of the train, I was not destined to sleep an entire night undisturbed. "Move, comrade!" The same conductor who had shown me to my place was now shoving me aside and opening the window above me. With the familiar stinging Siberian air pelting my back, I turned over and tried to sleep.

As the train neared Moscow the next afternoon, I realized that something was wrong—seriously, painfully wrong. I stood to walk to the train toilet, and as I did a daggerlike pain stabbed through my back. By evening when the train reached Moscow's Yaroslavskaya Station, I could not stand. Hunched over with the most excruciating pain I had ever experienced in my life, I dragged myself toward the dark street to search for a taxi.

"I just came from prison. I don't have any money to pay you, but I will ask my family to pay when we arrive at my apartment," I assured the taxi driver, uncertain whether I still had a family. "Don't worry," the taxi driver said when we were inside the cab. "I'm not going to take money from you, comrade. I only came from prison myself a few months ago."

This God-sent taxi driver helped me get into the elevator and walked with me to my apartment and rang my doorbell. "Meet your guest," the taxi driver said when my brother Styopa, who happened to be at the apartment that weekend, opened the door. Unable to stand erect to experience the moment for which I had lived three years, I now bent into Styopa's embrace. "My dearest sister! Lubasha . . . my darling sister." Strong Styopa wept, and I could feel his tears wetting my face as he shouted my name, nearly as hysterical as I had been in the Marinsk field.

The taxi driver who had lingered for this moment of reunion, perhaps reminiscent of his own, started to weep and pulled a wrinkled handkerchief from his pocket to cover his face. Neighbors from the four other apartments on our floor, perhaps the same people who had seen me taken three years before, peered through their doors, and a few even started to move cautiously toward me.

But it was my sensible Zhan who, startled by Styopa's wailing, had run to the door and was now prying me from my brother's arms, lifting me into his own and carrying me inside our apartment. Zhan's arms shook as he lay me on the bed and for the first time since I had known him, my handsome husband wept. "You've gotten a little gray." I stroked his temple and tried to smile through our tears.

"*Mamochka, Mamochka!*" Seven-year-old Vladislav tore through the bedroom door, landing beside me on the bed with a thud that shot darts of pain up my spine, but I pulled him to me through the agony, kissing his face and fingers. I clutched Dunya and twelve-year-old Ira who had entered the bedroom together. My fifteen-year-old son Lyonya entered last and sat shifting on my bed, touching my arm, waiting for my attention.

"Momma! Where's Momma?" I exclaimed, trying to embrace my entire family at once.

"She has gone to the Crimea to Evpatoria with your sister Ira, for a vacation. Don't worry, Lubasha—about anything," Zhan soothed, pulling a blanket around my shivering shoulders.

"I must have a shower!" I exclaimed. Zhan and Dunya removed my prison uniform, helped me to the shower, and when I had washed, dressed me in the pink brocade Japanese robe I had worn the night of my arrest.

"You must try to sleep, Lubasha," Zhan insisted. "We shouldn't try to talk now. I will leave you so you can sleep." Feverish and fitful, I knew that Zhan was right. But why, when I had never known a day of illness in the prison, should this night of delirious happiness be destroyed by pain? A fury rose inside me, pushing away any gratitude that my illness had at least happened among people who loved and cared for me. Tears of rage rolled down my cheeks and I turned from Zhan. Even he didn't understand. How could he think of leaving me for a minute, I sulked.

"Dunyochka, Dunyochka!" I cried when Zhan had gone. My nanny came scurrying to answer my summons as she always had, and I buried my face in her lap and wept. *"Dytynka moya, dytnyka moya,* . . . my little child," she murmured in Ukrainian, stroking my head. And despite all my strength and self-reliance I knew Dunya was right. At least for that night, I wanted to be a child.

When Zhan returned to our bedroom I still had not fallen asleep. His fingers groped for mine across the bed and then we threw our arms around each other, shaking the bed with our sobs. "I've sent a telegram to Evpatoria to Ira," Zhan said when he had again settled me in bed and sat stroking my hair as gently as Dunya. "Ira will tell Momma that you are home."

The next morning I awoke to find Zhan watching me. How haggard, how much older he looked, I noticed with a shock that made me wonder how my sufferings had altered my appearance. Soon Dunya was in our bedroom bustling about me, plumping my pillow, worrying if the bed had enough blankets. And then the children, rosy-cheeked and healthy, were circling my bed, setting up little tables beside it. "Auntie Dunya said we could eat breakfast in here with you, Mamochka," Ira said, snuggling toward me. Dear God, how could my family know what a shock well-fed children, pressed linen sheets, and a real bed were to me.

"Who is Auntie Dunya's best helper?" I asked, pulling Vladislav to me. "Irochka, wouldn't the blue ribbon look best in your hair with that dress?" I asked, trying to break down the barriers of three years by speaking as nonchalantly as if I had never been away from my children at all. But it was Lyonya—now fifteen years old—who worried me the most with his scrutinizing looks that followed me everywhere. And every time I hugged him, he stiffened.

"He is a teen-ager now, Lubasha," Zhan said when I fretted about Lyonya's behavior. "Just give him time and he will understand," Zhan added vaguely. "You know the things they teach them now at school." With a pain worse than the stabbing in my back, I understood. Communist cant about "enemies of the people" was drilled into every school child. How had my children's teachers categorized me?

"Do the children's teachers know I was in prison?" I asked Zhan.

"You must be patient, Lubasha. I tried to do my best. But we must be cautious . . . It takes time, you see," Zhan murmured and then swiftly switched the subject to the present. "The first thing we have to think about this morning is your passport. I need to register it immediately at the militia office."

"It's on top of the desk with my release form," I said, motioning to my rosewood desk in the corner of our bedroom. Zhan picked up my passport and studied it. When he turned toward me, his face was white.

"What is it? What is the matter?" I exclaimed, starting to stand and walk toward him, but a burst of pain in my back sent me staggering back onto the bed.

"This passport!" Zhan clutched the document which I had not even bothered to examine when it had been issued to me in Marinsk. "That minus six, Lubasha. Do you know what that means?" Zhan stammered, the small piece of paper fluttering in his trembling fingers. "Minus six means the authorities have deprived you of the right to reside in six of the capital cities of the Soviet republics, and of course that includes Moscow. Legally you are not allowed to spend more than three days in Moscow!"

And that was how we discovered that the terror which I had thought I would shed as easily as my prison uniform had somehow followed me home. Zhan embraced me and we both wept, not the heaving sobs of yesterday, but helpless, hopeless silent tears. "You've got to leave, Lubasha," Zhan was saying. "It is too dangerous. The MGB could use this as a pretext and come back and rearrest you tomorrow."

"But I can't leave you and the children and Dunya and Momma—I'm sure she and Ira will run back to Moscow the minute they receive your telegram," I cried.

"I'll tell Ira everything, and she and Momma will come to you in Sochi," Zhan said, stroking my hair. "You must trust me, Lubasha. I want you to go to the Goncharevs in Sochi, where you will be safe. I must stay here. I will work every minute to have your passport changed and then come to you as quickly as I can. You know how sunny it is in Sochi. It will be just the medicine for your back," Zhan insisted, trying to find courage for us both. "You know how kind the Goncharevs are."

The Goncharevs, a couple we had met during vacations in Sochi, could not have been kinder, helping me limp from the comfortable couchette which Zhan had reserved and making me feel at home every moment in their comfortable, spacious brick house, which also served as an office for Sergei Petrovich Goncharev and his three sons, who were all dentists.

For three months I lived with the gracious Goncharevs—three months as calming and healing as the vast Black Sea visible from the Goncharevs' terrace. Every day brought reassuring calls and letters from Zhan and new waves of kindness from my hosts—fresh oranges from a Greek ship which had docked in Sochi that morning; visits from the Goncharevs' sympathetic friends to cheer the poor sick political prisoner recuperating in their home. "You are looking more like yourself every day, Luba Leontievna. You will be back in ballet yet!" Sonya Stanislavna Goncharev, a handsome woman with bright, black eyes, would say as she carried books, food, and the latest local jokes to my bedroom.

The only comfort the Goncharevs withheld from me was information about my mother—the same subject about which Zhan had been so vague. Although I inquired each day and sometimes several times a day for information about my mother, it was only when I was nearly well enough to leave Sochi that I learned the truth. Momma and Ira had not gone to Evpatoria for a holiday, but so that my mother could recover from a heart attack precipitated by my imprisonment.

Now the doctor feared the news of my release might cause another attack. It was the doctor who had forbidden me to contact Momma, and my poor family and the Goncharevs had been forced to conspire to keep the truth from me. "You were so ill, Luba Leontievna," Sonya Stanislavna explained when she finally told me the truth about my mother. "Zhan was afraid you couldn't bear the news. We wanted you to recover from your illness first."

In prison I had concentrated my strong will on survival. Now I bent every fiber of that will, which I credited with saving my life in Marinsk, to getting well. I would be well. By the time I was, Zhan would have procured a passport for me. I would be able to visit my mother and Ira in Evpatoria. I stretched my back toward the healing afternoon sun streaming on the Goncharevs' terrace and tried to think positive thoughts.

Because the compassionate Goncharevs had concealed all unpleasant facts from me as long as they were able, I did not learn until the last month of my stay with them that my fugitive flight had not quite ended, even in Sochi. Sochi, it seemed, while not one of the minus six capital cities, was a city legally closed to dangerous political prisoners like me. Not until I returned to Moscow did I learn that the Goncharevs had bribed militia officials with what local parlance termed "vodka money" to enable me to recuperate safely at their home.

On June 21, well enough to travel sitting upright, I returned to Moscow for a homecoming shrouded by the news that Zhan's frantic efforts had not procured permission for the change in my passport which would permit me to live in Moscow. "Zhan, will I ever be anything but a fugitive?" I moaned as I lay in his arms, both of us listening for footfalls which could signal the end of my freedom.

"You should return to Sochi or go somewhere even safer, Lubasha," Zhan said, his tight embrace belying his suggestion that I again leave. "Moscow officials are stricter than those in Sochi."

"I can't leave . . . I won't leave," I wept. "Now that I am well enough, I'll go to the militia myself and beg them to change my passport."

And I did go to every militia office in our district. Often I visited the same offices several times and frequently I was shunted from one office to another. From those officials who would receive me, replies ranged from disinterested to discourteous, but they always added up to the same hopeless logic. My passport had been issued in Marinsk. Therefore, the only possible way to have it altered was to return to Marinsk. But as most of the militia officials candidly conceded, there was no assurance the militia office at Marinsk would change my documents either.

By July 20 Zhan and I had visited all the militia offices in our district several times, except the one which was reputed to be most closely controlled by the MGB. "Maybe it will help if you go there yourself, Lubasha," Zhan said heavily.

On the morning of July 20 I joined the large waiting room at the militia office, full of citizens who seemed as weary and wary as I. I waited until nearly noon when I was summoned into the office of a militia official who continuously glanced at his watch. When I told him my story, he shrugged his shoulders and said,"The only way you can change your passport is to return to Marinsk. But nobody in Moscow is going to give an order for the authorities in Marinsk to do that. But you had better leave Moscow," the official instructed, impatiently ushering me out of his office. "If you stay in Moscow illegally many more days you will probably be arrested."

Outside the militia office a drenching summer downpour beat on the pavement. The official's warning about being arrested clung to me as I hurried home through the rain and entered my apartment, my spirits as sodden as my clothes.

Dunya set steaming tea from the samovar before me, and Zhan settled me in my ballerina chair. I silently sipped the tea, unable to tell them about my disheartening visit. "Lubasha, do you believe that dreams have significance?" Zhan said suddenly, breaking our silence. "Vladislav woke up this morning after you left for the militia station, crying from a nightmare. In his dream he saw you and me sitting on the moon. Suddenly the moon split-and you and I floated away in different directions. Whatever happens now, Lubasha," Zhan said holding my hand, "we won't let them separate us again."

Vladislav had also told his dream to Dunya, and she scolded Zhan as she refilled our glasses with tea. "You shouldn't scare the child by telling her such things," she said, hugging me and crying.

Exactly one hour after Zhan had told me about Vladislav's dream, Dunya was settling the children around the dinner table. The chimes from the antique clock in our hall, a wedding gift from my Bolshoi colleagues, had just struck six when our doorbell rang. I raced to the door, flung it open, and, as I had known from the moment I heard the doorbell ring, the *bête noire* was there. Two MGB officers and a policeman in uniform pushed into our apartment. "They're here!" I screamed.

Zhan ran toward me, slamming the dining room door to protect the children from the terrible scene. Through the door I heard Dunya wail, one long measured cry like the mourners I could remember at Grandfather Kentrszhinsky's funeral. I started to turn toward the dining room for one last farewell. But then I stopped. At least I could spare Dunya and the children this last agony. I seized my summer raincoat from a hook in the hall and kissed Zhan swiftly, not permitting myself to cling to him. I stepped into the hall, and before Zhan could speak the policemen had slammed the door in my husband's face.

14 CHARON'S FERRY

How many times in my life had I performed the same play, the same dance, roles rewarded with applause and shouts of bravo, encore! Now, mechanically, I was once again repeating a performance, the worst role I believed life could call on me to play.

Again MGB officers were seated beside me in the car speeding me, the prisoner, to the Lubianka with all the urgency of an ambulance. And then the officers, relieved to be rid of their dangerous cargo, were pushing me out the door, marching me through the prison gates.

A seasoned actress, I could predict the sequence of scenes in this ridiculous replay: the body search, the fingerprinting, the somber march through the stone halls scrupulously cleansed from the contaminating possibility of contact with other prisoners, and the cell, not the same number as before, but otherwise identical.

Numbly I plodded through the motions of my agonizingly familiar role, too frozen at first to feel the harsh hands of the two women guards who searched my body and ripped away the gold necklace Zhan had given me for my birthday.

By the second morning in my old role, I had begun to thaw; and as feeling returned, along with it came a steely determination to survive. With this mental sword, welded during my first term, I would slash my way into my second.

My first foray came that morning when I was summoned for interrogation.

The interrogator, whom I had not met before, was clearly bored by too many performances of the same act. He yawned as I entered the door and regarded me with less attention than the slow-burning cigarette he held in his hand. He laid the cigarette in a brass ashtray and shuffled through a stack of papers on his desk. "Luba Leontievna Bershadskaya, your previous sentence was an error. Only three years for spying for the Americans is a ludicrously light sentence for a crime of that magnitude," the investigator inveighed, warming to his role. "However, the *troika* has reviewed your case and noted its error. Your sentence has been extended to an additional ten years," the interrogator announced in a tone that seemed to signal I ought to be grateful that justice had triumphed.

In seconds, almost to my own surprise, I was striking back at the interrogator, my bold swashbuckling words ringing through the room. "I was naive when you arrested me the first time three years ago," I shouted. "Then I stupidly believed you were decent people who would free an innocent person. But now I know you are not human! You are scum, and it is beneath me to speak to you!"

"Don't worry, we have ways of extracting information, prisoner." The interrogator stressed the last word, looking not at me, but at the cigarette butt he ground to shreds in the ashtray beside him.

"*Ya plyuyu na vas!* I spit on you!" I screamed, but before I had the opportunity two guards stood beside me, pulling me from the room back to my cell.

The next morning, wise in the protocol of Lubianka, I leaped to my feet at 5:30 A.M., still longing for sleep after the previous night's interrogation, but prepared to spend the day sitting stiffly on my stool.

A guard peered in my cell. Checking the new prisoner, I thought grimly. He won't find anything to fault me.

But to my astonishment the guard, an old man whose face I could scarcely see in the dim light, was motioning me back to my bed. "Sleep a little longer, prisoner. I won't tell," he whispered.

And so once again I had encountered a guard with heart and kindness which MGB monsters had been unable to destroy—a thread, thin as it might be, which helped prevent me from losing all hope in humanity.

In two days I was transferred to Lefortovo, the prison constructed by Peter the Great, famous under the Soviets for its reputation of extracting confessions from the most recalcitrant prisoners.

At Lefortovo, a silent guard motioned me inside a cell, so tiny that the other prisoner had to sit on her bed to permit me to enter.

The other prisoner, Luba Ivanovna Polyakova, was a beautiful woman with large, languid blue eyes, now the most prominent feature on her thin sunken face. "And so you are also Luba." She reached a frail hand to greet me when the guard was safely gone and we had introduced ourselves. "I'm sorry to have such poor quarters to offer a guest," she said forcing a flicker of humor, when I discovered that I could only walk three short steps between our two narrow, metal beds.

But it was delicate Luba Ivanovna who needed cheering more than I. Luba had been arrested three months earlier for consorting with an English army general, for whom she had left her Russian husband. Like me, Luba's contact with the British general and other foreigners stationed in Moscow during the war had supplied the Soviet *troika* with an automatic verdict of espionage.

Luba and I spent seven months together immured in our cell scarcely larger than a tomb, interrupted only by signals from the mummylike guards who handed us our food, led us to the toilets, and marched us down the mausoleumlike corridors to interrogation sessions.

I, older and more experienced in ways of prison than Luba Ivanovna, wanted to help this gentle, bewildered young woman who reminded me so painfully of my own initiation to prison three years ago at Lubianka. "We spoke only of love, never politics." Luba Ivanovna would plaintively recite the chronology of her affair with the general. If she could convince me of her innocence, she seemed to believe, somehow the interrogator could also understand.

Each day Luba Ivanovna and I received the same meager, unappetizing rations—two pieces of bread and kasha. Every day I gave her a large portion of my bread. "At first they tried to starve me into confessing," Luba told me one day when I was worrying about her rapid weight loss.

When she was first arrested, the authorities had given Luba almost no food for fifteen days. One night a guard summoned her to an interrogation. Inside the interrogation room she found her interrogator seated before a sumptuous table laden with cakes, fruit, and caviar. "Prisoners who don't confess are lucky to be fed with even black bread," the interrogator had sneered, proceeding to eat before the starving Luba.

Those seven months of trying to help and instruct Luba Ivanovna perhaps benefited me more than her. But there were, of course, days when my own load crushed me. Although I was interrogated only five times during my seven-month incarceration at Lefortovo, I recoiled from the stuck-needlelike repetition of every session: "You're a spy! A traitor! It's a tragic miscarriage of justice that you should have been handed such a light sentence!"

At Lefortovo I was always summoned to interrogation at night. I did not dread the wearisome interrogations nearly as much as the trip to the interrogator's room which led past a row of rooms Luba Ivanovna and I called the torture chambers. Although neither she nor I had been inside these rooms, we could plainly hear the screams coming from within them. Returning from my own comparatively mild interrogations, I could not sleep with the hideous cries from the torture chamber hanging in my memory.

In Lefortovo, Luba Ivanovna and I seldom met other prisoners. It was only later in Siberian prisons that I met some of the prisoners whose wails I had heard through Lefortovo's walls.

Anna Andreyevna Kuusinen was one prisoner who survived Lefortovo's tortures only to be sent to Siberia where I later met her in Kengir Prison. Anna Andreyevna spoke eleven languages and had, before her imprisonment, often been sent by the Kremlin on diplomatic assignments.

It was contact with the world outside the Kremlin which first stirred doubts in Anna, who had been a devout Communist from the days of the Bolshevik Revolution.

When she was arrested in 1947, Anna knew that her real crime was to have seen enough of the world to be certain of Soviet corruption. When she would not confess to charges of anti-Soviet treason, Lefortovo interrogators summoned Anna Andreyevna's husband to give evidence against his wife. Threatened with imprisonment himself, he repudiated Anna.

One night in Kengir Prison in Siberia, a woman physician who occupied a bunk near me was summoned to treat a new prisoner with two broken arms. "The authorities' only worry is that they won't be able to assign the poor soul to a work brigade," the doctor grumbled.

The next morning the woman with the broken arms—Anna Andreyevna—was ushered into our barracks. Anna, excused from work until her arms healed, kept to herself, spending most days sitting on her bed, staring.

One morning a male guard entered our barracks for an unannounced inspection. All of us prisoners stood except Anna Andreyevna.

"Why aren't you standing, enemy?" A strapping young guard with gleaming boots strode over to Anna's bunk.

"Why would I rise to show respect to you? You aren't worthy to wash my boots!"

"What's your name?" the guard snapped.

"That's none of your business either," Anna Andreyevna replied in a surly voice.

Close enough now to see Anna's limp arms, the guard asked, "What's wrong with you? Do you have artificial arms?"

"They are broken," Anna screamed uncoiling her feet. "The idiot interrogator at Lefortovo broke them when I threw a chair at him."

"How dare you slander an honest Soviet Communist!" the young guard shouted, his face flushing.

But before he could say another word, Anna Andreyevna was hurling herself toward him, kicking him in the groin. The guard staggered back and lurched to seize Anna. In seconds we other prisoners grabbed her like a flour sack, shoved her under a bed, and formed a cordon before the furious guard who finally retreated through our barracks door.

We managed to hide Anna Andreyevna for almost a day, ignoring the guards' threats that our fate would be worse than hers.

At the end of the day, Anna ran from her hiding place screaming hysterically, "It's an earthquake! We're perishing!" In seconds two guards had her in their hold, dragging her by her broken arms through the barracks door. Weeks later we learned that she had been committed to an insane asylum for prisoners.

For the hundreds of indifferent, inhumane prison officials and guards that I encountered, there were always a few who had retained remnants of humanity and who must have hated their jobs. A little more than two months after my second arrest, Luba Ivanovna and I met such a guard in Lefortovo, a place which seemed sealed with a plaster mixed especially to block out any drop of human kindness.

On September 30, the day of faith, hope, and love, the name day for both Luba Ivanovna and me, she and I occupied ourselves with creating a bouquet of flowers out of squares of toilet tissues we had hoarded.

A young guard who had not spoken to us before peered into

the cell and whispered through the door, "What are you doing?"

"It's our name day!" I said gayly. "We're both Lubas. That means love, you know."

The guard stepped away with no reply, but a few hours later returned with two small dishes of kasha sprinkled with a few slivers of meat. "Greetings on your name day, girls," he whispered, shoving the extra food into our cell.

On January 15, 1950, in the dead of a winter as bitter as Moscow can bring, I was summoned with no time for anything but a swift good-bye embrace to Luba Ivanovna for the second act of my hideous repeat performance.

There were a few variations in the choreography, of course, but the overall plot and props were so painfully similar that I hardly noticed. There was the same brutal winter cold and the same chain of endless black boxcars waiting to cart us to hell in a trip that must have made Charon's ferry across the Styx seem a pleasure cruise.

It was only when I had stepped into a cattle car still redolent with manure and realized that this box, bursting with ninety-two other women political prisoners, was to be my home that I appreciated the comparative comfort of my first trip to Marinsk with only five other women in a compartment which had at least previously been inhabited by humans.

And our final destination? That uncertainty we prisoners also accepted as supinely as sheep. "Do you know where we're going?" I stood close to a woman beside me, whose body shook in deep, rhythmic shivers.

"I don't know and I don't care," she said dully. There was an indisputable logic in her words. What difference did it make to which of the Siberian prisons we were being taken? Unlike Dante, we had passed the point of compartmentalizing hell.

On my first trip to Marinsk, all the other women had been like me, first-term prisoners not yet past the point of trying to find some thread of sense in the tangled skein of their lives. Now the ninety-two of us women crowded in the cattle car discovered that we had all been in prison before. Our new misfortune, we concluded, was part of the mass arrests of 1949 when the MGB had corraled nearly all former prisoners. If we had been guilty before we must still be guilty, the reasoning went. Beyond that perfunctory exchange of information, our despair left us little to discuss.

There were only the daily routines of prison transport trains to keep us alive, such as the trips to the slop bucket, weaving one's way through slumped bodies. Each day we shifted places so that everyone could experience a few hours by the snow-encased windows which provided our only view of the outside world. Meals—a foul-smelling boiled cereal concoction—were pushed each morning into our car after the guards counted heads to insure that extra bowls would not be sent in for prisoners who had died during the night.

It was the relentless cold blowing through the slatted sides of the cattle car which was primarily responsible for the death toll in my car—fifteen women in thirty days. I would wrap myself in memories of Sochi's sun and try to recollect how fortunate I was to have recuperated so completely before my second arrest and to have even gained some extra weight. Less fortunate was my lack of foresight in preparing a satchel of warm clothes and food for prison when I had known I might be rearrested. Now, clad in the same light maroon cotton dress I had worn the day of my arrest and my raincoat, I huddled against other bodies as eager as I for our shared warmth.

A small kindling stove with a shriveled chimney stood in the center of our cattle car, a sight which at first sparked hope among us of a fire and warmth. When no fire was built we prisoners pled and then taunted, "You probably built a fire every day for the cattle!" One day, toward the end of our trip, a more merciful guard threw some kindling and matches to us. We gratefully built a small fire and its warmth seeped through our car, blocking the bullying cold but also burning oxygen and lulling us into blissful sleep—a sleep so deep we nearly died.

I awoke to find myself stretched on a snowbank with other prisoners spread prone alongside me. Guards were slapping and shaking us and cursing. "You idiots! How dare you try to suffocate yourselves!"

"We'd be better off if we *had* all died," a woman ten years younger than I moaned when the guards had shoved us back into the car. "Don't say that!" I chided, trying to rub some feeling into her frostbitten hands.

"You're so strong," the girl whined. "Not everybody has your strength you know, Luba Leontievna."

My physical stamina I could attribute to ballet. But during those awful days on the train I felt another power flowing through me more strongly than any force I had ever experienced. A glint of insight about its source came to me in a dream I had on the train.

In the dream I was a woman, but still somehow a child, walking beside a kindly man whose features I could not see clearly. It was his voice that was memorable. "Look! Look, Luba Leontievna! I've brought you here to look and to learn. You don't understand now but you will. Every minute of your life has meaning. There is a purpose for everything."

When I awoke from my dream I thought of the old Christian woman I had met at Marinsk—the only person I had met in prison with faith sufficient to see purpose and pattern in her suffering. "Maybe God was speaking to you in your dream," one voice inside me suggested. "Maybe it's your own will," another voice whispered. "Hasn't prison taught you yet not to rely on anybody but yourself?"

"In everything I seek to grasp the fundamental." I thought of the line from Pasternak's poem. For me the fundamental was survival. I had survived three years of prison. Somehow, I vowed, I would live through ten more and I would not just live. I would arm myself with an arsenal of facts which I would somehow lay before the world. I would have my revenge. Such resolve fueled my strength to survive.

But my fierce resolve often flickered, and on some days the flame I had so carefully fanned seemed close to dying. What are you but another heap of rags in this boxcar? a part of me mocked myself. You are a midget lashing at a monster.

On most days, as our cattle car jolted toward Kazakhstan, I refused to succumb to such pessimism. Instead, I forced myself to concentrate on my three-pronged plan. I would survive. I would share my strength with others. And someday I would record for the world all the horror I had seen.

Unfortunately for my grandiose plans, there were seldom opportunities to see beyond the four walls of our railroad boxcar. Occasionally when our train stopped in switchyards filled with other prisoner convoys, the guards would permit us to open the doors of our car wide enough to watch what was happening outside. One such scene permanently imprinted itself in my mind.

From our boxcar I saw a small convoy of women prisoners standing in a clump near our train. One of the women held a frail boy with pale cheeks by the hand. We women in the car, many of us mothers ourselves, watched as a soldier approached the little boy, patted him on the head, and handed him a piece of sausage. "Can you sing me a song, little man?" the soldier said.

The child hesitated a moment and then in a clear, high voice that carried into our car sang the only song his short Soviet childhood had taught him: "Thank you, Comrade Stalin, for a happy childhood . . ."

15 KENGIR

On February 15, 1949, one month after our departure from Moscow, our cattle-car convoy arrived in the central Asian wasteland of Kazakhstan. We who had survived the trip stumbled from our cattle car onto a snow-covered field, stunned by both the dazzling sun reflecting on the snow and the stinging subzero winds which wracked our thin bodies.

During the thirty-day trip we had been permitted no contact with the twenty-five hundred men on our train, all political prisoners sentenced to twenty-five years. Now the guards herded them onto the same field where we women stood. When the men spied us, they surged toward us, ignoring the shouts of the armed guards, "Halt! Halt! We'll shoot you all!"

In minutes the men had surrounded us, forming a fortress and shielding us with their bodies, pulling scarves, stockings, and sweaters from their own bedraggled bodies to help warm ours. A giant, gray-haired man whose shoulders convulsed with shudders of cold handed me a pair of stockings. I grasped his hand and then embraced him, with tears in my eyes. Through the clamor I said, "I'm a ballerina with no stockings to keep my feet warm. You've given me the best gift money can buy in Kazakhstan," I jested, afraid we would both be weeping.

"Women over here! Men over there." The guards, their orders unheeded, attempted another strategy. But the men, separated from their own wives and mothers and sisters, refused to be separated from us. Some instant chemistry of common consent fused us together as if the guards did not even exist. Resigned to the impossibility of separating us, the guards now prodded us, "Move fast or we won't reach the prison before dark!"

We walked fifteen kilometers in three hours, sustained by the men beside us who covered us with their clothing, supported us when we stumbled, and—when the guards were not looking—half carried the weakest among us.

Whipping winds blotted out the prison until we were within yards of the black brick walls and squat barracks rising like some hellish kingdom on the landscape before us. Outside the prison gate two officials, wrapped in fur parkas, had set up a table with a stack of dossiers on new prisoners. Four guards held the papers so they would not be blown away by the wind, and while we women waited, trying to shelter ourselves, the male prisoners were first summoned before the officers.

After two hours an officer strode out from inside the camp and grunted at the two officials seated at the table, "What are these women doing here? We can't process women here. They are supposed to go sixty kilometers further to Kengir!"

Without the warmth of the men we women shivered together, too weak and frozen to discuss our fate. "I will die if they make me walk sixty kilometers," a woman beside me wept. However, in minutes three trucks appeared and we women were loaded onto them.

As the trucks sped through weather which had now become a blizzard, the icy wind dug into our bodies with fifty times the force we had felt walking. "Why didn't they let us walk?" some of the women moaned. Others shrieked and howled until the sleet and snow gagged their throats.

It was already dark when we arrived at the camp. I heard guards unhooking the rear gate of the truck and snarling for us to step off. Too frozen to move, we hung back until the guards hurled us to the ground. I lost consciousness until several hours later when I found myself in a warm barracks with a woman prisoner beside me, spooning warm tea into my mouth.

Later that night all ninety-one of us women were transferred to Kengir's prison hospital, where we stayed for a merciful week of warmth, rest, and slightly increased food rations. But even the hospital could not remedy the ravages of our terrible transit to Kengir. During one week forty of the women who had survived our train trip died in Kengir Hospital.

I emerged from the hospital, still haggard and exhausted, to survey my new home, Kengir Prison Camp, its low-slung barracks sprawling like an enormous black spider across the snowy steppe. Kengir, while depressingly similar in appearance to Marinsk, was considerably larger, with a population of eleven thousand men and twelve hundred women. The women's camp was separated from the men's by a distance of about a hundred yards. Through the center of this no-man's-land stretched a ten-foot-high mud-brick fence topped with barbed wire spikes. The women's camp and the three sections of the men's camp were each surrounded by another mud-brick and barbed wire fence. One wide gate provided the only outside exit from both the camps.

Thus, one hundred yards of land and one wall was all that separated us women from the male prisoners with whom we were permitted no contact, since even our exits from the outside gate were timed to never coincide.

Nevertheless, the proximity of the male prisoners' camp was felt by us and provided strength and solace and even a spark of romance. One day I overheard Dunya, a lovely Ukrainian girl with golden hair the color of Kiev wheat, fretting about our shapeless black uniforms with our prison numbers imprinted in four places. During the few hours we had been with the male prisoners on the march to Kengir, Dunya had met Viktor and convinced herself that he had been transferred to the camp adjoining ours. "What if we meet by the gate some morning and Vitya sees me in this ugly smock?" Dunya would say, indulging herself in her implausible daydreams.

While still in the hospital I had been allotted a prison uniform and number—CSH 776. While in the hospital, I had also met other inmates from Kengir who had given me glimpses of what to expect from my new home. "Everybody works at Kengir," Lena, a veteran of six years in the camp, whispered to me one night when the guards had gone. "The bosses aren't as cruel here as in some of the other camps, but that's because they want to keep us alive to work. They divide the prisoners into brigades," Lena said. "Each brigade has a leader, a prisoner who is supposedly chosen by the other prisoners to oversee the brigade work. The authorities always make sure that the meanest women are chosen for this task," Lena warned.

Three days out of the hospital I was assigned to a brigade

which worked in the quarry, led by Dusya, a name I had already heard bruited in the hospital as one of the most cruel brigade leaders. That morning I joined the black bands of prisoners exiting through the gate, and did not pause until my brigade had slogged eight kilometers to a stone quarry.

Dusya, a hulking woman with a stupid stare, beckoned us to a tool shack and handed each woman a huge, heavy pick. When she placed the pick in my hands, my weakened body crumbled to the ground and the pick fell from my hands. I lifted myself up, perspiring with weakness from the long hike and the heavy weight of the pick. Suddenly, startling even myself, I began to laugh uncontrollably. Prisoners beside me edged away, hissing, "She's lost her mind."

Still laughing hysterically, I collapsed on the ground with Dusya towering over me. "I won't, I can't do this work," I said, cradling my arms about me and rocking in the snow to keep warm.

Dusya shrugged and said, "They must have made a mistake. You shouldn't have been assigned to the quarry. We can't waste all day watching her," she said, waving the other women to their work.

All that day I sat in the snow, struggling to keep warm, grateful for Dusya's unexpected understanding. It will be all right tomorrow, I kept consoling myself. They will assign me some work inside the camp.

That night when our brigade had straggled back to camp, I decided to forego our gruel supper and climbed onto the wooden bunk which I had been assigned to share with two other women. Before I could bury myself in sleep a guard was shaking my shoulder, summoning me to the office of a camp administrator.

Seated in a chair, his feet on the desk before him, the administrator did not stand when I entered, but shook a piece of paper at me. "Dusya reports that you are physically capable of working at the quarry, but too lazy to do so," the administrator charged.

"It's a lie! I'm too weak for that work," I replied, slumping against the wall.

"Stand up straight!" he shouted, rising from his chair. His voice also rose. "You didn't come here to have a good time, you prima donna. You came here to work!"

Not flinching, I took two steps toward the administrator. "The first time you arrested me, I was naive and frightened," I said coldly. "But now I know with whom I am dealing, and I know my strength. I'm not afraid of you and your kind any longer, and you won't force me to do anything against my will!" I shouted as I stalked from the room.

Full of fury, I marched back to my barracks and, before I had taken many steps inside, spied the gorgon Dusya seated on her bunk. I grabbed her by the lapels of her jacket and banged her head against the wall. Swarms of prisoners surrounded us, but no one came to Dusya's aid. Somehow she finally managed to crawl from me, leaving my hands clutching her coat.

A new shaft of hatred shot through me and I lunged toward Dusya, grabbed her by her hair, and threw her to the floor. I stomped her face with my feet, ignoring the blood streaming from her nose. Finally the prisoners pulled me away from her, and a prison doctor appeared and carried Dusya away.

The next morning Dusya was transferred to another camp and I, after a sleepless night, was summoned before a prison officer. "So these are the actions of a refined lady, a highly educated Bolshoi ballerina," he sneered.

In truth, although still seared with hatred for Dusya, I was horrified at the murderous rage which had seized me. "You've taught me to behave like this," I answered. "If it weren't for you, I would never have sunk so low as to treat another human being in such a way," I added.

"You are not in the Bolshoi now or the American Embassy, my fine lady," the administrator taunted.

"Unfortunately that is true," I said sarcastically.

In Marinsk prisoners had been dispensable. In Kengir every particle of human labor was needed, and it was to that necessity that I credited my reassignment to another job without more penalty than the rebuke from the administrator.

My new assignment in the laundry meant I did not have to leave the camp. It also meant that I, who had never washed one article of clothing in my life—at home Dunya even washed my stockings—was now assigned to scrub two hundred pieces of soldiers' underwear every day.

Fearless as I had been since arriving at Kengir, I now resolved to make the best of the laundry, which, however loathsome, was preferable to the quarry, the fishing cannery, or the building construction crews on which many women prisoners worked.

The first morning I entered the laundry room punctually at 6:30—a long, cold hall with a cement floor bordered by built-in tubs so low that one had to bend almost to the floor to reach them. In the center of the room on a slightly elevated stove stood another row of metal tubs filled with boiling laundry. As I stood surveying this scene, a woman in her early twenties approached me. I turned toward her, struck instantly by her beauty. "Who are you?" I exclaimed.

In one breath she replied, "I am Lida Beasova. I am an artist and sculptor from Moscow. I was arrested because I wanted to marry a French pilot."

As readily as Lida had confided in me, I told her my story, and that day—the first day in the laundry for us both—produced a friendship between us that continued during my time at Kengir.

Lida, whose life in Moscow had been as pampered as mine, hung back, helplessly watching the strapping Ukrainian farm women who bent over the tubs near us. We noticed that two women shared one tub and before Lida and I could be separated, we found an empty tub and swiftly set to work.

By the time Lida and I, equally inexperienced, had figured out how to squat by our tub, a slender woman with an aristocratic appearance entered the room. "It's the laundry manager. Her name is Emilya Navdysh and she is the wife of a famous Latvian artist," Lida whispered.

I studied Emilya Navdysh as I scrubbed. "Such an intelligent face—I don't think she will be cruel," I observed to Lida, recollections of the obtuse Dusya still vivid in my mind.

By noon I had washed only a quarter of my pile of underwear and Lida less. At noon we stopped for only seconds to fill our bowls with soup and then stooped back over our tubs. "Look how fast my soap is disappearing," Lida moaned, examining the small sliver of soap in her hand. "The Ukrainians told me it's the allotment for the whole day."

I tried to develop a rhythm to rub more swiftly, but the extra effort only burned my back muscles and chafed my hands, which had already begun to bleed.

After scrubbing the gray shorts and shirts, we had to carry them to the stove and boil them in the pots before we retrieved them for rinsing. "Thank goodness, at least we can straighten our backs long enough to walk to the stove," Lida groaned.

By six o'clock that evening, the Ukrainian women had finished their work, but Lida and I still faced two heaps of underwear. "Goodbye, intelligentsia," the Ukrainians tittered as they left the room.

Emilya, who had scarcely spoken to us that day, stopped beside our tub. "You can't leave until you finish your assignment," she announced. I finished about 9:30 and worked until 11 o'clock to help Lida. We staggered from the laundry, our bodies feverish and aching. Without undressing, we threw ourselves on our bunks and instantly fell asleep.

In the night I awakened and realized that Lida, who slept on a bunk near me, was gone. I leapt up and discovered her sitting, sobbing in a corner of the barracks. When I approached her, she lifted her face and I saw that her luminous brown eyes were red from crying. "It's Emilya," she wept. "She came to my bunk and pulled my hair to wake me up. When I awoke she was standing over me, her face twisted with anger.

" 'You trash! Look how you washed these clothes. You dirtied them instead of getting them clean!' she screamed, and then she started slapping my face with a wet undershirt she held in her hands. You know I tried, Luba Leontievna." Tears tumbled down Lida's lovely face. "I did the best I could."

I whirled from the barracks, not caring that it was against the rules to leave the barracks at night. I stormed into the laundry room where Emilya both worked and slept, jerked two soggy pair of men's shorts from a tub, and lashed Emilya in the face just as she had done to Lida.

"Stop! Have mercy! I shouldn't have hit Lida!" I feared Emilya's bloodcurdling screams would wake the whole camp. She tore herself from me and cowered behind a cupboard.

Somehow Emilya's screams shook me to my senses, and I was able to shed enough hatred to feel some pity for the cringing creature before me. I started to sob, still angry at Emilya, sorry for Lida, and ashamed and trammeled by my own terrible temper.

Finally, like the cultured women we had once been, Emilya and I started to speak sanely and we talked until morning, with Emilya pouring out to me her troubles in trying to please the camp authorities, who continually demanded greater production from the laundry. "They take it out on me, Luba Leontievna, if the quotas are not filled. You know they always extract the work somehow. As it is, I often have to stay up half the night to finish the work."

By morning I found myself sympathizing with Emilya, but nevertheless insisted, "You must apologize to Lida."

Although Lida and I eventually learned how to wash our two

hundred pieces of underwear in a reasonable time, the backbreaking chore did not grow easier. Like Sisyphus, the legendary king of Corinth, we were condemned to roll a heavy rock up a hill in Hades only to have it roll down again as it neared the top. No matter how swiftly we pushed through our pile of laundry, there was always a new mound awaiting us the next morning, frequently larger than the day before.

For two years this situation continued until one night, throbbing with pain, I fell on my bed, buried my head in my hands, and wept. Now it was Lida's turn to comfort me. "I don't care what they do to me. I can't bear this torment any longer," I wailed to Lida.

Despite Lida's cautions against such an action, the next morning I marched to the camp administrator in charge of work assignments. "I'm not a horse. I'm a human being, and I refuse to step inside that laundry one more time," I huffed.

The officer, his face as red as the epaulets on his jacket, stormed toward me screaming, "You lazy bourgeoise ballerina! You've gone too far this time! You're going to solitary until you come to your senses. If you won't work, you won't eat!"

And that was how I found myself confined for six months in a cell the size of two telephone booths, attended by mute guards who thrust my food—one cup of water and one small piece of bread—through a chute in my cell door once a day. My only human contact occurred during my daily trip to the toilet when I was escorted by a guard. Otherwise, I had to content myself with swift glimpses of the hands of the guard who shoved my rations into the cell. For two months the same thick, calloused, clumsy hands performed this task. Then one day the hands were drastically different—thin, trembling fingers with long nicotine-stained fingernails. I distracted myself for hours trying to picture the rest of the person that belonged to the hands.

I entered solitary in January with Kazakhstan's winter at its worst. The first three months of my confinement I paced the tiny perimeter of my cell, stomping my feet to stay warm. For those first three months I could not sleep on the cement floor, but with spring the cell became more bearable.

As the weather turned warmer, a mustard-colored spider appeared in one corner of my cell and assiduously spun a web. I spent hours engrossed in the spider's effort and felt a certain desolation when he emigrated to another cell. For sanity's sake I knew I could not permit myself to dwell disproportionately on such diversions. Prison lore was filled with stories of people who had lost their minds over less.

I remembered Viktor Eremyeyevich whom I met in Marinsk. Sentenced to be executed, Viktor was placed in a solitary confinement cell for eight months. All that time, he had no contact with other prisoners except for their voices, which he sometimes heard as they were being led to their execution. "Good-bye, comrades!" they sometimes shouted, refusing in the last moments of their lives to be muffled by the guards. But even that sound ended when the guards began gagging prisoners on their way to be shot.

One day a fly entered Viktor's cell. Viktor spoke to the fly and made sure the insect did not depart the cell through the chute which the guard opened daily to deliver Viktor's food.

Finally Viktor was summoned from his cell. Sure that he would be executed he bid the fly good-bye. When he reached his destination a surly officer informed him, "Your sentence has been changed to twenty-five years. You may go to the prison barracks."

But Viktor did not walk toward the barracks. He fled back instead to his cell screaming, "The fly! The fly. I must free the fly!"

The best way to survive solitary, I had learned from my nine months in Lubianka, was by harnessing my strong will to the task of survival. Like a plow in a straight furrow, I dared not permit my mind to ramble. There was a certain pattern of positive thoughts that must be pursued.

Before my release from solitary a catastrophic event occurred which made all the prisoners' lives slightly more livable and brought hope to those of us who were politically literate.

"Stalin, our noble leader and heroic friend, is dead," Kengir prisoners were informed by guards with mournful countenances. Some guards—and prisoners—wept. Many prisoners secretly danced and laughed.

The evil king was dead. An epidemic of hope swept among the prisoners, and the news reached even me. Now surely sane men would triumph. With the terror ended, we would be released. But, to our terrible dismay, no mass pardon ensued.

One change which seemed significant did occur after Stalin's death. All numbers were removed from the uniforms of political prisoners, and guards began addressing prisoners by their names. By the time I was released from solitary, I was once again Bershadskaya rather than CSH 776.

In what appeared to be a small wake of leniency following the tidal wave of Stalin's death, another remarkable event occurred in the Kengir Gulag.

About sixty kilometers from our camp was the Dzhezkazen Prison of the Kengir region, located next to the large oil wells of Dzhezkazen. This camp, populated entirely by male political prisoners, was reputed to be the most squalid in the Kengir region.

Unexpectedly, in the summer of 1953, officials from Moscow visited the camp and spoke to a convocation of prisoners. "If you work well, you will be paid, food shops will be set up, and your sentence will be reduced. We know how to value labor," the authorities announced, leaving the prisoners, whose labors had been despised for years, to reel at such a radical statement from the bosses. A year passed and to the astonishment of the prisoners the Moscow authorities, desperately anxious for increased oil production, kept their word.

When the Moscow delegation returned in a year, the prisoners—emboldened by the revolutionary changes which had already occurred—raised a new demand. "There is a women's camp sixty kilometers from here, and we know there are women there who were once famous artists. We request you to permit the women to present a concert for us."

To the astonishment of the prisoners, the authorities granted the request; and the next day I was among the twenty-five women prisoners selected to participate in the concert. At our first rehearsal I was chosen by the other women to direct the performance.

On the eve of the concert, all twenty-five of us paced up and down our barracks with our hair rolled up in paper curlers. Despite numerous discussions on how to beautify ourselves for the concert, we had not been able to overcome the greatest obstacle, our shapeless black prison uniforms. When we had requested permission from a woman warden to wear civilian clothes for one night, she recoiled in horror. "Your whole identity depends on those uniforms," she averred.

Despite the dreadful uniforms, on the summer day of the concert we felt imbued with a sense of identity and dignity not experienced by most of us for years. In the morning, when the truck arrived from Dzhezkazen to transport us the sixty kilometers to the men's camp, one of the performers, Elena Konstinova, nudged me gaily. "Look how clean the truck is, Luba Leontievna. The men must have prepared it especially for us!"

We stepped onto the truck clutching our hopes and, carefully concealed from the convoy of ten guards who accompanied us, several slips of paper with names and addresses of male prisoners. As soon as the word of our performance at Dzhezkazen filtered through the women's camp, other prisoners had come to us performers with names of husbands, brothers, and sons. "Try to help us find them," they pled. Among us we had accumulated about five hundred such names.

When our truck was still a few kilometers from the Kengir men's camp, we spied crowds of men. And as we entered the gate the thunderous quake of cheers sounded as if all twenty-five thousand prisoners had come to greet us.

Through the commotion, sounds of a Strauss waltz drifted to us from a small welcoming orchestra somewhere in the crowd. Like an army, the prisoners had formed themselves into two wide rows leaving only a narrow corridor for us to pass through to the dining hall where the concert was to be held.

We moved through this lane single file, with our convoy of guards trailing behind. I was second in line and, like all the women, was engulfed in the esteem of the men who had longed for this reunion as earnestly as we. From both sides of the corridor men kissed our hands and clung to them, reluctantly releasing us to the others. I began to weep but would not take my hands from the men to wipe the tears which streaked my face.

When our procession had ended, the men swiftly filed to their places in the dining hall, and we women were escorted behind the curtain of a crudely constructed stage. The sight that met us there brought a new torrent of tears. Twenty-five small tables had been carefully placed backstage and on each table were a mirror, makeup, a package of facial tissue, and a chocolate bar. We women, already tearful, began to wail. "We must stop this," Nina Evgenievna, one of the more sensible among us, insisted. "We musn't let the men hear. They will think we are ungrateful."

"They know, they know, Nina Evgenievna," I said, weeping myself. "Unlike our own husbands and brothers and sons, they can cry with us."

Our convoy of guards, who had been greeted with hoots and hisses as they passed through the corridor of prisoners, now grimly stationed themselves backstage to guard us during the performance. But before the curtain opened Yanosh Leonas, a Latvian poet, hurried on stage. "We prisoner workers demand an immediate removal of the convoy," he said, addressing the prison officials who sat in the front rows. "This is an insult to us. We will guard our women," Yanosh cried to an avalanche of applause from the other prisoners.

The authorities in the front rows huddled together like a soccer team. Finally one functionary stomped backstage and reappeared leading the convoy, who like shamefaced schoolboys slumped into seats in the audience.

I was the mistress of ceremonies, and although I had choreographed several of the dances and coached the dramas I did not sing or dance myself. Starved as they might have been for art, the men were far more starved to see our faces and they applauded wildly after every act, bringing each performer back for at least two encores. I had scheduled the program for each performer to have a few minutes to introduce her act. How we women labored over those few words, selecting and revising, forcing each word to carry an impossible weight.

When the performance had been extended as long as the authorities would permit, Yanosh Leonas, spokesman for the male prisoners, strode again to the stage to invite us women to dinner.

The dinner, served on the stage, had been carefully organized by a committee of prisoners to permit us maximum contact with as many men as possible. Even though soldiers had reappeared to guard us while we ate, we knew that our opportunity had come to inquire about the five hundred names we carried. Therefore, while we exclaimed over the incredible feast the men had prepared—white bread, meat, cutlets, apples, and lemonade—we passed our slips of paper to the men and probed for information to carry back to camp.

After the dinner, the entire audience was readmitted to the theatre and the gracious Yanosh Leonas again appeared on stage.

"Now, our dear sisters, we have prepared a surprise for you, and I have the honor of making the first presentation," he said. With that announcement Yanosh lifted a large plywood box from the side of the stage. "These gifts are for the Latvian women here and back at camp. We Latvians send these tokens to our women with this message: Dear wives, mothers, sisters. You are always in our hearts, and they break with your suffering and pain."

Yanosh was succeeded by a parade of speeches and gifts to us from other nationalities—Ukrainians, Estonians, Lithuanians, Russians, Finns, and Uzbecks. Remembering Joshua who prayed and the sun stood still, I wished I possessed such power to extend this day, holy to both the men and us. But after the men's final presentation our guards, who themselves seemed solemnized by the events of the day, reluctantly led us back toward our truck. Again we were flanked by the men who sang as we passed through the narrow corridor, a song then popular in Moscow:

> *I love you under the moon,*
> *I love you because you are near,*
> *I love you because you are you,*
> *Good-bye, good-bye, the night is approaching.*

16 REVOLT

In the months following Stalin's death in March 1953, the reins of the chariot of state clutched so tightly by the dictator seemed to slacken slightly, and we in Kengir welcomed the change. But by autumn 1953 we prisoners, practiced at sniffing the wind, scented a shift for the worse.

As the spring of 1954 approached, both Kengir's captors and captives sensed the rumblings of revolt. Fearful the volcano might erupt, the captors tried two new tactics. In March and April of 1954 several contingents of political prisoners, whom the authorities viewed as most contaminated and therefore most likely to lead strikes, were transferred to other camps. At the same time the officials began dumping criminals into Kengir, a prison which had been almost entirely populated by politicals, innocent victims of Stalin's purges.

"Maybe you cultured gentlemen can reform your less fortunate brethren—if they don't kill you first," one lieutenant colonel sneered when the first contingent of criminals was injected into the men's camp. The criminals, the authorities calculated, would make life so miserable for the politicals that they would have no time for incendiary thoughts of rebellion.

By May Day, the officials had injected seventy-five criminals into Kengir's male prison. Now under attack not only from prison officials, but also from the criminals, the desperate politicals formed a plan. "There are eleven thousand of us and seventy-five of them," Ivan Semyonovich, a ringleader among the political prisoners, asserted, rallying the other politicals around him. "Why should we sit back and let them bully us?"

Thus, for one of the first times in the history of the Gulag, the politicals of Kengir resolved to go on the offensive against the criminals. "We can whittle weapons and wield them as well as you and there are a lot more of us!" the politicals warned the criminals. "Think it over. Would you rather cooperate with the MGB bosses or with us?"

Although most of the worst plunders stopped after this warning, the criminals' propensity for breaking rules did not, of course, disappear. On a suffocatingly hot Sunday in May, several of the criminals exerted their energies on a new escapade. Most sacrosanct of Kengir rules were those forbidding any communication between cordoned sections of the prison—the three sections of the men's camp and particularly between the men's and women's sections.

On Sunday morning, May 16, a band of criminals from section three scaled the twelve-foot wall between sections two and three of the men's camp. Warding off the prison guards who tried to pull them away, the criminals from section three hurled stones and mud bricks at their pursuers and succeeded in entering section two of the men's camps.

In Kengir, in order to provide a respite for prison guards, Sundays were nonworking days. This meant a maximum of prisoners inside the camp and a minimum of guards. Captain Belyaev, security officer in charge of section three, summoned reinforcements to stop the criminals, but when the criminals finally retreated back to section three on their own, the officials shrugged the incident off and hoped that the remainder of Sunday might pass undisturbed.

But the restless criminals had only been sparked by the success of the morning, and around noon the volcano erupted. With homemade slingshots the criminals shot out the lamps, which burned even during the day, around the boundary zone between sections two and three of the men's camp. With the experience of the morning's exploits behind them, they swiftly scaled the wall and dropped into section two—the section nearest the women's camp. In minutes they were surging toward the most forbidden and therefore the most enticing conquest of all—the hundred yards with a ten-foot mud-brick wall topped by two feet of barbed wire which separated the men's camp from the women's.

With a wooden beam, the criminals rammed their way through the fence of a service yard of section two bordering the hundred-yard stretch between the men's and women's camps. With the same wooden beam and shovels and picks from the service storehouse, they tunneled a hole through to the women's camp. At this point some politicals joined the criminals, believing they should come along to protect the women.

That Sunday noon I was lying on my bunk, fanning myself with a newspaper, trying to find some relief from Kazakhstan's heat. Two women wardens, the only guards in sight, sat outside our barracks visiting.

Suddenly this Sunday calm was rent with the sounds of shots and voices of men inside our compound screaming, "Strike! Strike!" I rushed from my barracks to discover bloody, screaming bodies hurtling toward us through the wall. Several of us women started pulling the wounded prisoners into our barracks, but soon the guards were on our side of the fence shouting at us to keep away from the wall and battering some of the women who moved closer.

"We've got to have doctors and nurses!" I shouted to the women who were trying to attend the wounded men inside the barracks. But the doctors, prevented by the prison officials, did not appear and the few nurses among us with the help of the rest of us women were left to help the wounded the best we could. We grabbed bedding and clothing and ripped it in strips to staunch the bleeding from the gaping, gushing wounds.

In an hour, when the camp officials had succeeded in sealing the flow of prisoners through the wall, they bellowed to all sections of Kengir Camp from loudspeakers posted on top of the boundary walls and in the towers, "All men must be out of the women's barracks by four o'clock or else they will be shot." Like bullets, this announcement ripped repeatedly through the camp.

Bands of guards had been dispatched into our camp and they patrolled outside our barracks, staring in our doorway, but could not enter through the barricade we women had formed with our bodies.

With the soldiers barred, we bent ourselves to treat the wounded, with no medicine, little skill, and the threat of the four o'clock invasion ringing in our ears. Through this maelstrom of misery, eddies of deathbed conversations swirled around me. "I beg you to send a message to my wife . . . Do you have a cigarette? . . . How many of our boys made it through the hole?" I sat stroking the arm of a young criminal whose straw-colored hair was matted with blood.

What strange alliances this war had formed. But there was no voice raised among the women in our barracks to suggest that we ought to return the men—mostly criminals—to the authorities at four o'clock in return for our safety.

About three o'clock, two other women and I asked the soldiers guarding our door for permission to walk to the outhouse in the courtyard. They waved us on and as we approached the outhouse, which bordered a section of the exterior prison wall, I noticed a small rolled-up piece of paper lying on the ground.

Certain that any move to retrieve it would attract the attention of the soldiers stationed along the wall, I fell in a feigned faint on the note and seized it. My two frightened companions, convinced that I had truly fainted, lifted me in their arms and carried me back to the barracks. Inside, I leaped to my feet and opened the note. "Don't be afraid! They will not shoot at four o'clock!" the note said.

To our astonishment, the mysterious author of the note, evidently a sympathetic soldier, was correct. At four our enemies did not invade as they had threatened, but instead lowered their guns and left the camp.

Were they waiting for instructions . . . for reinforcements? We could not know, but through the bloodshed we exulted in our freedom. When the soldiers did not return, several other women and I ventured into the courtyard and edged cautiously toward the wall. Emboldened by the soldiers' departure, a new stream of men— mostly politicals—were now creeping through the tunnel in the wall, battering it wider so that more could come through at the same time.

In their haste, some of the men scaled the mud bricks to leap over the top of the wall, but from their towers the authorities saw what was happening and flicked on the electricity in the barbed wire rolled along the top of the wall. The men who had reached the top fell electrocuted from the wall like flies, and we on the ground screamed hysterically trying to warn the men on the other side who could not see what was happening.

Not content with this slaughter, the soldiers in their towers began shooting at the prisoners crawling through the hole. The men who had not been hit pulled the wounded through and handed them to us to carry to our barracks.

"We need you in the barracks to help with the wounded!" Lida was tugging at my sleeve, her cries releasing me from the paralysis with which I had been stricken by the horror at the wall.

I stumbled toward her. "You pick up the feet. I will lift the head," the once-fragile Lida ordered, bending over a wounded prisoner whose stomach had been gutted into a bloody crater.

"What can we do? We've got to have a doctor . . . We've got to dig the bullets out . . . There's no room for the wounded . . . We have to carry out the dead." Inside the barracks a chorus of cries from my frantic comrades met me. Delirious as I was at that moment, I realized someone must take charge. "We've got to stop the bleeding! Cut up everything you can find—even your uniforms! Boil water in the mess hall!" Like a general, I reeled off orders to the women in my barracks, trying not to faint as I walked through the rows of mangled men writhing and screaming with pain.

At nightfall the shooting stopped, and men poured through the hole in the wall into our camp. I grabbed the first men I saw who were not wounded to carry dead bodies from our barracks. This grisly trek continued all night until the dead—at least one hundred men—were transported from the barracks.

Besides the cessation of shooting, the greatest blessing nightfall brought was the arrival of Dr. Fuster, a Spanish prisoner who was a surgeon. Two other doctors arrived that night through the wall from the men's prison. Fuster took charge, mobilizing every medical person, and dispatching others like me to boil water and carry supplies from a storehouse which had been broken into by the prisoners after the soldiers' departure.

The storehouse was not the only building broken into that night. The solitary confinement block, where I had spent six months, was one of the first targets. Using wooden planks from bunks and railroad ties, our men smashed the walls, freeing the hundred women inside. That night several men also sketched a sign on a sheet which they unfurled between two posts in the prison courtyard. "Freedom or Death!" the sign read.

War had been declared in Kengir, and even as we worked that night to try to save the battle's casualties, our fury forged itself into a battle plan against our enemies. In the middle of the night, the prisoners without wounds and the wounded who could walk assembled in the prison courtyard, the groans of the injured and the stench of their wounds drifting toward us through the stultifying warmth of the summer evening. A political prisoner, the German engineer Yuri Knopmus, mounted a stack of lumber and addressed the crowd.

"The MGB murderers have mowed down hundreds of innocent men! We must strike! We must agree not to go to work tomorrow or the next day or ever until a commission from the Central Committee of the Communist Party in Moscow comes to investigate and punish our murderers." Yuri harangued until he was hoarse, shouting above the roar of the prisoners, who were screaming, stomping, and applauding his words.

17 SUPPRESSION

Sunday night was the first of many sleepless nights. Soon all time became dislocated, the days and nights mingling together in a new calendar in which such distinctions had lost significance. After years of the same repetitive camp rhythms, the symphony controlled so strictly by our captors had collapsed into cacophony.

Although we lived in terror of invasion, the officers, guards, and soldiers who had slunk from our camp after four o'clock on Sunday afternoon did not return, but retreated to the safety of guard towers around the prison's outer walls. The battle lines are drawn, we prisoners assured each other; the enemy surrounds us, but we hold the camp. Armed with a wooden club, Yuri Knopmus shouted to the crowd of prisoners perpetually around him. "The MGB murderers are not stepping foot in this camp, brothers—except on our terms. We demand that a member of the Communist Party Central Committee meet with us!" Yuri, with all the fervor of the commander he had suddenly become, rallied his troops around him.

On Monday the cautious enemy did not try to enter the camp, but from their strongholds and loudspeakers on the wall boomed a volley of messages toward us. "Prisoners must report to work as usual . . . Prisoners must report to work . . . If prisoners report to work as usual, a commission will meet with all prisoners to consider prisoner demands . . . Prisoners must report to work as usual."

These announcements, ignored by the majority of prisoners, by Tuesday morning nevertheless created a commotion among us. Yuri Ilitch, a political prisoner in the final month of his ten-year sentence, began a crusade to convince the rest of us to return to work. "We're crazy if we think we can resist. You know they'll crush us one way or another. At least they are willing to talk. I think we should take their terms while we can. I'm going to work!"

A few prisoners agreed with this reasoning and trudged out the gates to work and, to our surprise, returned safely inside Tuesday evening—full of assurances of goodwill from the bosses. "They promise they'll listen to all our grievances if the whole camp returns to work tomorrow!" Yuri Ilitch exclaimed.

"You idiots! You traitors!" Like tinder, the wrath of the many prisoners who had stayed inside the camp exploded on the few who had gone out. "You know the MGB swine are liars! You've betrayed us all!"

And thus, tragically, on the second day of Kengir's strike, the enemy nearly succeeded in dividing us. Even more tragically, it was the intervention of the enemy that finally brought us to our senses. The verbal attacks on the prisoners who had gone to work swiftly turned to a fistfight in the men's section. Some men began to strike each other with the wooden weapons they had made to fight the officials. The officials, observing every movement inside the camp through binoculars, saw their chance to strike and fired from a tower into the group of prisoners.

Their feud forgotten, the prisoners fled, and on Tuesday's sleepless night we shuddered at how nearly our cause had been lost through anarchy. We could not afford discord and disunity. Inside the prisoner-controlled Kengir, there must be law and order.

It was Misha Keller, a Ukrainian partisan and a veteran of strikes in Koloyma and Norilsk, who urged us to action. "If the bosses find out we can't run the camp, they'll be on top of us in minutes! We've got to elect a commission and set up committees and run this place in an orderly fashion."

We twelve thousand victims of lawlessness seized Misha's proposal for law and order like starving men. "We hate the way the MGB stooges run this place. Let's show them how a decent society should be run!" Thus we prisoners, our own rulers inside the confines of the camp, organized ourselves into the longest-lived strike in the Gulag's history.

We first elected four men, all with previous experience in prison strikes, to be our leaders: Yuri Knopmus, Misha Keller, Gleb Sluchenkov, and Anatoly Kuznetzov, a former first lieutenant in the

Red Army. Next we tackled the day-to-day administration of the camp and laid down a few basic laws. "There will be no debauchery. If any man harms a woman, he will be killed," Yuri declared explicitly enough for every criminal to understand the edict.

The restraint of a second decree decided that day later amazed many of the chroniclers of Kengir's famous strike. "There will be no raiding of officers' food from the storehouse," Yuri declared. "We will appoint a committee to ration food from the supplies in the storehouse already designated for prisoners. Our rations will be increased, but we won't touch the officers' food. They're the thieves—not us! Let them keep their white bread and chocolate and butter—may it choke in their throats!"

Besides legislating camp laws, we also established several committees with such titles as defense, technical, internal security, and food and services. "At least we will be washing our own underwear and not that of the MGB," Lida said to me. Lilliputian as our weapons were compared to those of the officials, we also set up a schedule for prisoners, paced thirty steps apart, armed with wooden clubs and metal bars from prison windows, to guard the six blocks of walls around the camp.

In addition to preventing any of the enemy from entering the camp secretly, it was also the duty of our sentries to prevent any prisoners from defecting to the enemy. And, unfortunately, we felt forced to turn one small barracks into a prison to detain such people.

All during our deliberations and every day during the strike, prison officials blasted loudspeaker announcements into the camp with the same basic message, "Return to work!" Other than the ubiquitous blare of the loudspeakers, for one week we had almost no contact with the enemy circled around us like vultures in the guard towers. Then one morning we suddenly saw ten airplanes buzzing in the sky above us.

Abruptly the loudspeakers boomed a new message: "A high level commission from Moscow is prepared to meet with you. All prisoners gather in the courtyard!"

Our motley but massive army of prisoners assembled at the gate armed with sticks, bars, halberds, and other makeshift weapons. "We're unarmed!" officials shouted as they approached the gate.

"You're not coming in until we search you to verify that for ourselves," one of our men shouted and the generals, almost all officials from Moscow in charge of the entire Soviet Gulag, meekly submitted to our search.

Inside our territory, General Gubin, MGB chief of Razakhstan's Gulag, addressed us through a megaphone, his epaulets gleaming in the May sun. "There are thousands of you. We can't talk to all of you. Choose a commission to represent you, and we will return tomorrow to negotiate with the commission. We have come to talk with you on friendly terms. We want you to tell us what has taken place, and we want to explain our position to you."

A shock of silence followed the general's amicable announcement. "We've won. They're going to treat us like humans," a woman next to me exulted.

Her trusting words struck me like a slap in the face. "You aren't friends!" I screamed at the generals. "You are beasts! We don't trust you and we don't believe you!"

Gubin shouted back to me, "Bershadskaya, since you have been in this camp, have any of us officials ever deceived you?"

"The issue is not me as an individual," I retorted. "I am only one of thousands, and we thousands do not trust you."

"We repeat our offer," Gubin stated, ignoring me. "We will return tomorrow at the same time to negotiate with your commission." That afternoon ten men and two women—Nusya Mikhailevich, an indomitable Ukrainian peasant woman, and I—were elected to the prisoners' commission.

After the election a woman from my barracks said to me, "Have you considered the consequences, Luba Leontievna? I know you are courageous, but you still have five years of your term left. The commission members will be the first to be punished when they break the strike, and they may hang another ten-year term on your neck."

"They won't break the strike," I snapped. "We will win!"

Every day our prisoners' commission met with the fifteen Soviet generals and faithfully communicated their proposals to the rest of the camp. Every day we repeated our demands. Those responsible for the murders on Sunday, May 16, must be punished. Prisoners should be permitted to work eight-hour days and be fed with rations befitting humans, not animals. The walls between the men's and women's camps must not be rebuilt, and there should be no bars on the windows of prison barracks. We must be permitted unrestricted correspondence and packages from relatives and periodic visits. Our cases should be reviewed.

Our every demand was met with the same response by the generals. "You must stop the strike and return to work."

More stubborn than the generals, we would not budge. "We will not return to work until our demands are first met. We insist that somebody from the Central Committee in Moscow come to meet with us."

While neither side moved in this tug of war, we prisoners nevertheless felt victorious to have brought the generals to the negotiating table where we could sit for even a few hours as equals with our masters who had bullied and beaten and despised us.

We did not surrender one meter of this tactical advantage, but spoke with candor and authority. "Why should we believe you?" I asked the generals one afternoon when we had arrived at one of the many impasses in our negotiations. "You have no scruples; you fall whichever way the wind is blowing. When Stalin and Beria were alive, you bowed and scraped before them. Now that they are dead, you discredit them. How can we reason with people like you who are two-faced about your own leaders?"

Unable to whip and torture us for such comments, as they were accustomed, the generals sat stone-faced, forced to listen to our accusations, and angrily ended each session with the same instructions, "You must first return to work before we consider your demands!"

After several sessions the generals appeared to accede to a few of our demands. "A fair trial will be held to judge the soldiers who shot innocent prisoners," General Bychkov from the Moscow MGB promised one day. "But, of course, such an event must be preceded by the end of the strike," the general added smoothly.

Misha Keller leapt to his feet shouting, "Don't talk stupidly if you want us to negotiate seriously. You know that not one of us will move a meter until the guilty officials are first punished for murdering our innocent men."

While Misha was speaking, a soldier entered the room and saluted General Bychkov. "Comrade General," the aide exclaimed, "the prisoners are breaking down the whole fence between the men's and women's camps! They found a large steel rail, and they are using it as a battering ram."

General Bychkov jumped to his feet and shouted to the aide, "Start shooting from the towers! Immediately!"

I was sitting on the other side of the table and without thinking leaped toward the general and grabbed him by the sleeves of his jacket. "Don't shoot! Don't you dare shoot!" I screamed hysterically, clutching his sleeves with all my strength.

He tried to shake me away, but by that time a crowd of prisoners, startled by our screams, had gathered at the door. Bychkov glanced at the group, far outnumbering the fifteen generals inside, and with his face streaming sweat screamed at me, "What do you want me to do?"

"Don't shoot! Don't shoot!" I kept screaming, clinging like a leech to the general.

"Don't shoot! Get out of here!" the general ordered his aide, hunching back into his chair when I had released him. I fainted and slumped to the floor.

When I revived, Nusya and some of the men from the prisoners' commission were leaning over me. I heard one of them growl at the generals leaving the room, "For each tear that Luba Bershadskaya has shed, we are going to drain a bucket of blood from you MGB swine!"

Almost every day more prisoners who had been wounded in Sunday's battle died, a terrible reminder to us on the commission of the mortal issues at stake during our daily negotiations. One suffocatingly hot afternoon our commission met outside in the courtyard with the generals. Dr. Fuster, accompanied by two men carrying a stretcher, walked by. Suddenly Fuster turned and motioned the men with the stretcher to the space between our commission and the generals. Fuster jerked the cover back from the stretcher, exposing the body of a young man about twenty-five years old. "He died five minutes ago," Fuster shouted at the generals, "and it is your fault! It was your guards who shot him from your towers—just like they shot down hundreds of others in cold blood!" When the generals, who had moments ago been acting so tough to us on the prisoners' commission, saw that a crowd had gathered to hear Fuster's speech, they fled in terror toward the prison gates. As they passed through, the prisoners began to scream, "MGB murderers! May you perish in hell!"

Suddenly a man stepped out from the angry mob. "Dear brothers and sisters," he cried over the clamor of the crowd, "I am a priest. Let us bury our brother according to our Christian traditions and rites. I will conduct the funeral service right here!"

Although more than two hundred of our wounded had died by this time and most—especially on the first day—had been buried with no ceremony, a murmur of respectful assent rippled through the crowd, and the funeral service that day became a symbol of our sorrow for all the fallen.

Witnessed by thousands, the priests recited the funeral liturgy of the Orthodox Church and concluded the ritual with the comforting words from a Psalm:

> *God is our refuge and strength,*
> *a very present help in trouble.*
> *Therefore we will not fear,*
> *though the earth be removed,*
> *and though the mountains be*
> *carried into the midst of the sea.*

This sacred ceremony of such consolation to us made our enemies, observing the event from their towers, apoplectic. "Stop this religious fanaticism! Stop your service immediately!" the loudspeakers blared, but we weeping mourners only sang more loudly the traditional Orthodox funeral chant, "Lord, have mercy . . . Lord, have mercy . . . Lord, have mercy." This chant taken up at our comrade's funeral continued through the entire night despite the furious attempts of the officials to disrupt our prayers. From childhood I had been familiar with the chant, but it had been years since I had thought of it or sung it. Now I wanted to clasp these words which I remembered my mother singing and cover myself with them.

Our masters, who had been accustomed to controlling every aspect of our lives, hated us for flaunting our newly found freedoms. It was not just the funeral service which rankled. It was every manifestation of free choice from us slaves who, according to the calculations of our oppressors, ought to have been purged from such presumption long before.

Like yeast, our new freedom bubbled and frothed and broke through the surface of our troubles and tenuous security.

Christians, suppressed and stifled all their lives in the Gulag, after the strike suddenly found themselves with a hall designated for church meetings and freedom to pray and speak freely of their faith. I was pleased for these people but, preoccupied with my activities on the commission, did not take time to attend their meetings.

A consistent policy of the MGB throughout the Gulag was to scatter prisoners of the same nationality. From the first day of our strike prisoners of the same nationality in Kengir, who had been dispersed in different sections of the camp, exultantly clustered together. The Ukrainians were particularly closely knit, bonding together to work and sing, recite Ukrainian poetry, and vow that they would never again permit themselves to be parted. During the strike several marriages occurred among the Ukrainians, performed by their own priests. Observing these ceremonies, I felt as much sorrow as joy for these couples who might only hope to measure their happiness in hours.

Twice during the strike I took time from my somber commission duties to help organize concerts, and while all the nationalities—Russians, Latvians, Ukrainians, Estonians, Chechens—danced and sang and recited poetry in their own languages, it was again the Ukrainians who composed the most poignant hymn:

On the hot steppes of Kazakhstan
The labor camps have been stirred up.
The wearied backs have been straightened
Because the time to groan has passed.

The festering sore has been split open
In a fit of sacred emotion:
We will never, no, never, be slaves
And will never again bear the yoke.

The blood of our brothers spilled in Kolyma,
Norilsk, Vorkuta, and Kengir
Has overflowed the cup of violence,
And united all the camps.

Today we make a solemn vow
To those who fell for freedom's sake
That we will never, no, never, be slaves
And will never again bear the yoke.

Down came the walls which divided us,
Joined once again are brother and sister,
Father and daughter, husband and wife,
Lass and young lad are embraced in a kiss.

The first outpouring of freedom
Has brought all the nations together.
We will never, no, never, be slaves
And will never again bear the yoke.

All our tongues became as one voice,
Every heart is bound by one faith.
Anxiously on the barricades
The lass stands watch with the lad.

Our song and our slogan uplifted
Is,"Freedom for all our dear land."
We will never, no, never, be slaves,
We will carry the fight to the bitter end.

This song became Kengir's anthem, a banner to bolster our spirits, which frequently sagged while we, like patients with a terminal illness, waited for our fate to unfold. Although I was daily becoming more pessimistic about the outcome of the negotiations, I refused to permit myself to be fatalistic before the other prisoners. "We may be doomed to die, but I'm going to live every minute of this freedom," Lida remarked to me one day during the strike.

"I'm not going to die. I refuse to let those monsters be the cause of my death," I retorted with my usual obduracy.

As the negotiations with the generals wore on with no settlement in sight, even the most stouthearted among us could not suppress fears. True, the strike had endured not only for hours and days but even weeks. But how long would the bosses tolerate this stalemate? Perhaps our strike was suicidal. That festering fear was a sore our enemies wanted desperately to exacerbate.

One day I noticed seventy men—whom I immediately recognized as thieves from section three of the men's camp—stalking toward the prison wall with long sticks in their hands. Although a trust and alliance, unprecedented in the Gulag, had been formed between us politicals and the criminals, I was nevertheless alarmed by this belligerent sight. I marched up to the prisoners and asked, "Where are you going?"

"It's the generals from the commission," one of the criminals replied. "They're gathering prisoners together over in section two—agitating them to defect. They've got no right to do that, and we're going to teach them a lesson or two!"

The criminals, as it happened, were right. On the first day of our commission's negotiations with the generals, the generals had agreed to our demand that they not speak personally with any prisoners except those on the commission. Nevertheless, if the thieves enforced this rule with violence, I trembled at the massacre which might ensue. An attack by prisoners could only provide a pretext for counterattack by the enemy.

"You wait here!" I ordered the criminals, who knew I was a member of the commission. "I'm going this minute to talk to the generals and order them to leave."

Doubtful about the outcome of my plan, the criminals reluctantly agreed. "We'll wait. We won't kill the generals—yet. We'll follow you and see what happens."

The thieves led me through the hole in the wall to the men's camp, and there, as the thieves had said, sat nearly two thousand prisoners in a circle listening to General Gubin. I marched up, stationed myself between General Gubin and his audience, and shouted, "Prisoners, disperse! You must not listen to the lies of the generals!"

Gubin, whom I had stopped in the middle of a sentence, shook his fist in my face and would probably have struck me had it not been for the band of criminals behind me. "How dare you interrupt me when I am reasoning intelligently with these prisoners!" Gubin shrilled. "Who do you think you are!"

Ignoring the general, I screamed at the prisoners until I was hoarse, "Disperse! Depart immediately!" As the politicals ambled sheepishly away, I still felt terrified by the threat of bloodshed. The criminals with their sticks and fury stood poised, waiting for the slightest cause to attack the generals. The only way a battle could be averted was to move the generals out of the camp as fast as possible, and I now turned my fury toward them. "Leave this camp immediately! You know it is against the rules of the commission for you to address prisoners." The outnumbered generals skulked toward the gate, escorted by the criminals brandishing their sticks and shouting obscenities.

During the first two weeks of the strike, the commission met with us nearly every day. By the third week, with the meetings moving nowhere, we met only twice. On June 22, the sixth week of the strike, we met with the commission for two hours of negotiations, totally unfruitful. Nevertheless, the generals repeated their customary injunction as they departed, "Consider our proposals. We are ready to meet your demands if you will stop the strike. We promise to return to discuss this further."

In our worst nightmare, none of us could have envisioned the hideous horror of their next return. On June 26, the fortieth day of the strike, the loudspeakers, which day and night repeated the same messages, at four o'clock in the morning suddenly shrieked a new one. "Attention, all prisoners! We are preparing to shoot! Attention, all prisoners! We are preparing to shoot!" With a thunderbolt blast, fire trucks burst through the prison gates, crushing our guards who tried to stop them. They tore through the camp, spraying boiling water in a hundred directions.

Prisoners in the courtyard bolted back into their barracks, and in minutes an onslaught of thousands of soldiers rampaged into the camp, breaking barracks windows and hurtling tear gas inside. In my barracks a stampede of screaming, choking women struggled toward the door.

As I stumbled into the courtyard, four Red Army trucks filled with soldiers armed with small tommy guns rumbled into the courtyard. A convoy of four tanks thundered in their tracks. As soon as the tanks appeared, soldiers inside the tanks and from on top of the guard towers—hunters mowing down prey with no place to flee—sprayed gunfire on the crazed prisoners in the courtyard.

Lida and I flattened ourselves against a barracks wall. Bullets, moans, and screams flew past us. "Dig trenches!" "We'll fight the tanks!" "Oh, God! I'm hit! I'm dying!" I shrank against the wooden wall clinging to Lida, but suddenly a tank swerved drunkenly in our direction. Lida and I hurled ourselves from the wall and in seconds the tank was crashing through the building, crushing the few elderly women who had stayed inside.

I fled from this circling, crushing tornado threatening to suck me into its center. As I scurried for shelter, a newly married Latvian couple, clinging to each other, stumbled and fell beneath the claws of a tank beside us, and I saw pieces of their mangled bodies caught in the barbed wire which the tank trailed behind it.

For what seemed a lifetime—but which I was to later learn had been twenty minutes—the carnage continued. When the tanks, with their vodka-braced drivers, had rolled back through the gate and the shooting from the guard towers halted, General Bychkov drove into the camp in a jeep, meticulously steering his way through the wreckage of bloody bodies. He shouted to his soldiers as he drove, "You are to be commended for your honorable work."

"We did this in the service of the Soviet Union!" some of the soldiers shouted back, saluting smartly as they marched through the gates, leaving their trophy of splattered, dismembered bodies at Bychkov's feet.

18 THAW

In that most hideous hour of my life, more than six hundred prisoners had been wounded and murdered and hundreds more, I later heard, went insane and were transported to psychiatric prisons.

When General Bychkov drove from the site where the massacre had occurred, a swarm of other officials entered the camp, including one who ordered Dr. Fuster to "save as many of the wounded as possible." I stumbled after Dr. Fuster through the rubble of broken, bleeding bodies, trying to help transport the wounded in makeshift stretchers to the prison hospital.

"I need you in the operating room," Fuster said to me when we arrived at the hospital. I staggered obediently after him. Inside the operating room, he handed me a mask and cap (which I have kept to this day), a pen, and a writing pad. "Try to write down the name of each patient before I operate," he instructed.

Many of the wounded were unable even to utter their names. Many others died holding my hand while they moaned the names of their loved ones. Some not as severely wounded implored me to contact their families. A few died with the word "strike!" on their lips, and one dying man laboriously charged me through stiff lips, "Tell the world about the heroes of Kengir!"

After several hours stooped over the dying, I straightened and as I did, I noticed a mirror in the room. I stood before the mirror and removed my surgical cap to find my auburn hair nearly gray. I shook my cap, thinking specks of powder must have fallen from it into my hair, but when I brushed my hair with my hand the color did not change. Then I remembered how my scalp had prickled and burned that morning. I, at thirty-eight years of age, had turned gray in minutes because of the Kengir massacre.

After thirteen hours in the operating room Dr. Fuster fainted and was carried away. I was standing, wondering how I could help the rows of patients still awaiting surgery, when I felt a pair of hands on my shoulders. I turned to face two soldiers. "You're coming with us, Bershadskaya!" one grunted.

The soldiers escorted me to an office near the main gate. Leisurely lounging against the wall stood General Bychkov, surrounded by twenty soldiers. "Ah, what have we here? A member of the prisoners' government," the general said with a smirk. And then, mindful, I was sure, of the time I had clung to his jacket to prevent him from shooting the prisoners who were enlarging the hole in the wall, the general turned to the soldiers and said, "This lady has a lot to learn! Teach her a lesson! I'll wait outside!"

When Bychkov had exited with most of the soldiers, the five who remained stepped toward me and began shouting, "You rotten beast! You scum of the earth! You strike leader! This bloodshed is all your fault!" I flinched, ready for the soldiers' blows, but as I did I noticed they were smiling and with a flash of understanding that made me weep, I understood. These soldiers were sympathetic to the strike—and to me—and the best way to help me was to carry out their charade convincingly. For ten minutes they stomped and screamed and cursed and clapped their hands to sound as if they were striking me.

I, overcome by this kindness, forgot to fulfill my role and scream with pretended pain. But when the soldiers led me out to Bychkov, my tormentor fortunately attributed my silence to fear. "Good work, comrades. The witch will remember this lesson the rest of her life!"

The soldiers silently escorted me to a small cell. Locked inside I found Nusya Mikhailevich, the other woman on the prisoners' commission. We were incarcerated in this room for twenty days while the authorities interrogated us, attempting to extract every detail of the strike. "How did you, a former ballerina, get mixed up with this dirty group, with this disgusting strike?" The interrogators tried to shame me into a confession.

But I refused to divulge any details of the strike and would only repeat, "The strike was the noblest act of my life. I am not ashamed of it for one second. For forty days we were free and human!"

"You may be heroes to the other prisoners here, but you are not heroes in the eyes of the government!" the interrogators sneered.

"All that matters to us is what the other prisoners think," Nusya retorted.

The only time Nusya and I were permitted to leave our cell was to walk to the bathhouse. On the way we passed the cells where the men from the commission were being held, and they could see us through the bars on their windows. "Ladies, how are you? Take courage!" they would call as we walked past. But one day when we walked past, the men called out, "Good-bye, ladies. We have been condemned to be shot!"

"You two are not worth the bullets it would take to kill you," the interrogator jeered one day to me and to Nusya, who also refused to talk. "We're sending you to Kurgan. You'll talk there; that is, if the criminals let you live long enough!"

Before the massacre of June 26, I had always, even during the most desperate days when I felt myself drowning in my miseries, clung to hope of survival, and I had never stopped believing in my own strength. But now the enemy's tanks, which had crushed so many of my friends, had also destroyed some part of me.

With an alarm which did not rouse me to action as it would have in the past, I slowly realized that I had lost my will to fight, and it was with that spirit in August 1954 that Nusya and I arrived at Kurgan, a prison eight hundred kilometers beyond Kengir, deep into Siberia, which held only the most dangerous, degenerate criminals and in which political prisoners had never been confined.

When we arrived at Kurgan, a strict security prison with fifteen hundred inmates, Nusya and I were shoved into a cell with seven women who seemed to have come from an illustration of Dante's *Inferno*. They stared with cunning eyes out of shriveled, jaundiced faces, and they swore with the vilest language I had ever heard. "Thank God we have each other," I said, clinging to the stolid Nusya.

On the train from Kengir I had confided to Nusya, "I'll steel myself to endure any suffering at Kurgan if I can only live long enough to see my family." After two days of Kurgan's squalor and profanity I felt myself in danger of dying. "I can't bear their language," I wailed to Nusya.

In Kengir both Nusya and I, as political prisoners, had accumulated credits to purchase food from prison supplies. We had not used our credits, and we decided to try to bribe the criminals with them. "If the prison director will permit us, we will use every one of our credits to buy you anything you wish from the canteen if only you will stop cursing," we promised.

To our amazement, both the director and the criminals accepted our proposition, and, to our relief, our cellmates began to refrain from their worst curses.

Not only our canteen credits, but several other factors helped forge a relationship between us and the criminals during the ten months we spent in Kurgan, which surprised even the camp officials, who considered their charges beyond rehabilitation. Fortunately for Nusya and me, our reputation as strike leaders—in a strike joined by criminals—had preceded us to Kurgan and engendered considerable respect among our cellmates.

But the greatest element in our relations with the criminals was the compassion we showed them. It started with the supplies from the canteen and continued when I discovered that I could divert them from cursing and fighting with stories. And thus began my career in Kurgan as a raconteur to a cellfull of thieves and murderers. With nowhere else to go and very few other diversions, the criminals—who constantly reminded me of ugly children starved for affection—sat around me for hours while I told them about my childhood and life in the ballet and theatre. The moment I stopped, they pled for more stories and plied me with questions.

It was my idyllic childhood, I think, which fascinated them most. "You had your own room? . . . Your mother gave you milk? . . . You had ten dolls with hats?" they inquired incredulously. One day I told them the story of how I met Zhan. Masha, a young woman with a grotesque body and gravelly voice, interrupted to ask if I had other boyfriends besides Zhan when I was a girl. "Of course, Mashinka," I replied, using the affectionate diminutive of her name.

She burst into tears and when I tried to console her, she wept even harder and said, "Nobody ever called me Mashinka."

Nusya seldom spoke, but sat quietly beside me, a constant moral support as I entertained the criminals. On the eve of Russian

Orthodox Easter, a guard summoned Nusya from the cell. Ten minutes later he beckoned to me and I followed, shivering with worry for Nusya. He led me to a room where, to my relief, I saw Nusya standing beside a large box. "Your friend needs your help to carry her box," the guard said.

Nusya's box was stuffed with delicacies from her Ukrainian relatives—two large loaves of Easter bread, a large Easter cheese cake, a cheese pudding, twenty-five colored eggs, and thirty plump oranges with a fragrance which made us dizzy. The criminals dived toward the package, but Nusya closed the top. "Not now. Tomorrow is Easter," she said firmly.

On Easter morning we spread a towel for a tablecloth on Nusya's bunk and placed our few makeshift dishes on top.

"*Christos voskres!* Christ is risen!" Nusya embraced me with the traditional Easter greeting.

"*Voistino voskres!* He is risen indeed!" I replied with the words I had heard from childhood. With the criminals beside us, we settled around our Easter table, but did not touch the food until Nusya had prayed.

A further blessing in the unlikely setting of Kurgan happened in May 1955, shortly before Nusya and I were transferred to another prison. I had not received a letter from home since my second arrest in 1949 and did not expect to receive one in Kurgan, where all letters were forbidden. One night an assistant warden summoned me from my cell and when we were alone in the corridor whispered to me, "Who is Irina Leontievna Starzhevskaya?"

"That is my sister!" I gasped.

"Here, read this quickly and return it to me. Don't say a word to anybody. Your sister probably doesn't know that letters are forbidden here."

"Where are you?" my sister Ira wrote. "We have heard that all political prisoners have been pardoned by special decree and are returning home, but where are you?"

Even before I left Kengir I had heard rumors of mass releases for political prisoners, but I had refused to believe them. Now Irina's letter filled me with a frenzy of hope. But Nusya, stoic as always, tried to caution me, fearing the fall which we both knew could so easily follow elevated hopes. "If it's true, we should be the first to hear," she said sensibly.

In July 1955 Nusya and I were transferred from Kurgan to Potyma Prison, west of Kurgan and twenty-four hours by train from Moscow. When Nusya and I stepped onto the train for Potyma, the guards asked us our names. As we gave them, the other prisoners in the coach overheard and began to cheer and shout, "Hurray! We salute you, heroes of the strike!" Later when we reached Potyma's women's camp we received the same enthusiastic reception as our names spread among the prisoners.

But I, Luba the leader, who had once thrived on adulation, hardly noticed the acclaim. I could not think of myself as a hero but only a physically, mentally, and emotionally exhausted woman, thirty-nine years old and prematurely gray.

In Potyma, which held about a thousand female political prisoners, both Nusya and I were assigned to a work brigade responsible for mending soldiers' underwear. Only the prospect of reunion with my family gave me the will to stagger through each day's work. As I mended I mentally replayed reels of my past life and often collapsed in tears with longing for my family. I was tired . . .

It was at this period when I felt weakest that several unexpected mercies sustained me. The first was a loosening of restrictions on letters from relatives, and I at last felt some link with my family from whom I had been severed so long. They wrote cautiously, relaying almost no news about themselves, but constantly repeating the plea, "Where are you? Others are coming home."

Another mercy, so incredible it seemed a mirage, happened on a shimmering day in May. On a Sunday—our one day off from work—the camp director suddenly appeared at my barracks and made the startling announcement, "It's a beautiful summer day, and the woods are full of lilies of the valley. You are free to go for an excursion to the forest if you wish."

In an instant we were standing outside our barracks in rows of five waiting for guards to escort us. "There's not going to be an escort. I trust you," the director unexpectedly announced, waving us toward the forest.

There were nearly a hundred of us, and from habit we first marched in our usual rows of five. But someone broke rank and suddenly all of us, like paralytics with newly healed limbs, began to skip and jump and hop. We spread out in clusters through the forest talking, laughing, crying, and stopping to feel the birch trees.

We bent to the forest floor carpeted with acres of lilies of the valley and gathered the flowers to us, placing them in our hair and our belts. We piled enormous bouquets in our arms and kissed the flowers and spoke to them.

When we returned from the forest that evening and were approaching the prison gates, we saw the camp director standing on the porch in front of his house. One by one we paused before the porch and each of us laid a bouquet of lilies at the director's feet.

Another mercy at Potyma was my meeting with Natasha, a cultured young woman from Vladivostok who had been arrested about the same time as I and also torn from a devoted family. She and I spent hours exchanging information about our families and pondering the meaning of every letter we received from them. Not only letters from our families but those of other prisoners were filled with talk of rehabilitation, releases, and returns of prisoners. A rumor even spread that the new Communist Party chief, Khrushchev, had denounced the "excesses" of Stalin at the Twentieth Party Congress. Every day Natasha and I spent hours talking, examining every piece of the puzzle, desperate to fit a picture together which would assure us of our release and reunion with our families.

During all my years in prison, when the prospect of release had seemed hundreds of miles down the road, I had carefully rationed thoughts of my family, fearful that I, like so many prisoners I knew, would lose my mind if I permitted myself too large a dose of such thoughts. But now, as our hopes for release rose, Natasha and I indulged ourselves in endless recollections and scenarios of reunion with our beloved families.

"Lyonya was twelve when I was arrested the first time. He is twenty-two now. Even little Vladik is already sixteen," I sighed, starting to weep. "Now their childhood is lost to me forever."

"Dear Lubasha," Natasha consoled. "Don't permit yourself such dismal thoughts. The children are not lost to you. From all you have told me of your dear Zhan, I am certain he has kept you constantly in the hearts of your children."

By spring 1956, Natasha and I had examined and analyzed every swatch of news from home until it was more worn than our mending and our nerves frayed from waiting for some official word from our captors.

On a sultry afternoon in early June the electrifying announcement we had so long anticipated finally reverberated through the camp loudspeakers. "Tomorrow will not be a work day! All prisoners are to report to the dining hall at eight in the morning to meet with a government representative from the Kremlin!"

That night no one slept. All night long our colony of one thousand women scurried about like an anthill stirred with a stick. The shower room to which we had access only every ten days was heated, and we were invited to use it freely. All night long we bathed and talked and planned and even primped—rushing around to find paper to fashion curlers to roll our hair. "Perhaps if we look like humans they'll treat us like humans," Natasha said.

The next morning, several hours before eight o'clock, women began to gather in the dining room. Some sat, others paced the floor, and everyone chattered to cope with the unbearable suspense.

Exactly at eight o'clock twelve men in business suits, scented with cologne, entered the dining hall and seated themselves under a huge painting of Lenin before a long table with a red cloth. We women straightened our uniforms, patted our hair, and waited in sudden silence.

The official at the center of the table coughed and slowly shuffled to his feet. He bowed slightly and began his speech. "I and my colleagues greet you. We have come to you, comrades, from the Kremlin with a message. Our government has recently learned that 99 percent of the political prisoners in Soviet prisons have not committed any crime, and our commission has come to rectify the mistakes that have been made. From this day on you will not be forced to work. Beginning tomorrow we will meet with each of you individually to review your case, and if you are innocent you will be released."

When the officials concluded this staggering announcement he added cordially, "Now I wish to invite any of you who have a specific complaint to come forward and speak with us." We women, paralyzed by this thunderbolt announcement, could not move. We sat stiffly, silently, staring at the men. "Come, come, don't be afraid," the official chided, as if he and his kind had never given us cause to fear.

I sat watching as a few women crept forward and timidly began to recount their experiences of beatings, starvation, rape, and endless brutality. One part of me wanted to rush forward, fall at the officials' feet, and plead for release. Another wanted to spit in the officials' complacent faces. Fortunately I sat in my chair, too numb to move.

Despite our suspicions, the next morning prisoners were summoned for interviews exactly as the officials had promised. Organized by work brigades, we were instructed to wait in a lobby while prisoners were called to appear individually before the commission. This process continued from eight in the morning until eight in the evening seven days a week. During the entire period, which lasted for three weeks, prison doctors, armed with tranquilizers, were stationed in the lobby to aid overwrought prisoners.

On the day following the commission's arrival the Potyma camp director unlocked the prison gates, and a stream of pardoned prisoners poured through them to a small electric train especially ordered to transport released convicts to the railroad station in the nearby town of Kursk. It was as if overnight Potyma Prison had turned into a college during graduation week. The majority of prisoners who appeared before the commission were granted an immediate release. Those who weren't were promised a further review of their cases. Every release called for jubilation and we whose names had not yet been called escorted the fortunate ones to the train for final farewells.

Natasha and I nervously awaited our summons to the commission. My work brigade was summoned before Natasha's. When I was finally called to come alone before the commission I, who had trained myself never to show fear before my captors, could not stop trembling before the twelve men who would decide my fate.

"For what crime were you imprisoned, Comrade Bershadskaya?" the chief interrogator asked when I was seated in a chair in the center of the room facing the twelve.

"I was not sentenced for any crime," I replied tersely. "I was sentenced on 'suspicion of crime' because I worked for the American Embassy."

The interrogators asked a few questions about the embassy and then the chief interrogator said, "If your story is true as you have told us, the charges against you will be dropped. But first we must send to Moscow for your dossier to confirm the facts."

At that moment I felt myself a runner felled within meters of the finish line. My whole body strained to win and I started to shake. "Please! Please!" I pled, discarding all my pride. "Don't make me wait until it is reviewed. It will take months and months for my dossier to arrive from Moscow. I beg you! Release me now!" I cried.

"Please calm yourself, Luba Leontievna," the chief interrogator urged, kindly addressing me by my formal name. "I promise Moscow will not keep you waiting."

In this month of miracles, Moscow dispatched a comparatively prompt reply. On July 20, 1956, exactly seven years after the date of my second arrest, I was summoned to meet again with the commission, which had by now moved three kilometers away to the men's section of Potyma Prison. That July a young woman guard who had been newly hired by the prison escorted me through the meadows and small village which separated our camp from the men's.

As we approached the administration building of the men's camp, I noticed many men seated on the grass outside the wooden hall. As I stepped closer I saw the somber expression of the men's faces. When my guard stepped inside the building to present my papers, the men swiftly surrounded me and I discovered the cause of their sadness. Only the day before, one of their friends had been pardoned from serving a twenty-five-year sentence. He had rushed out from the administration building to share his joy with his friends and fell at their feet, dead from a heart attack. Now as my guard returned to usher me into the building the men called, "Good luck, Luba Leontievna! Calm yourself!"

I was escorted to a chair in the center of a room with a painting of Lenin, which seemed an exact replica of the room used by the commission at the women's camp. The chief interrogator greeted me cordially and immediately stated, "I am happy to inform you, Luba Leontievna, that we have received your papers from Moscow. All charges against you have been dropped. You are free to return home to Moscow. We congratulate you!"

At that moment I who had not permitted myself a moment of weakness during the forty days of Kengir's strike slumped forward in my chair and felt as if I might faint. "Thank you . . . thank you . . . thank you," I kept saying softly, clinging to the words to keep me conscious.

Finally one of the officials rose and stood beside me. "May I help you?" he asked me politely, offering me his arm and assisting me to the door. When I appeared at the door on the arm of the official, the men seated on the ground leaped forward to snatch me from him.

Supporting me among them, they seated me on the ground and put a cup of water to my lips and a cold wet cloth on my forehead. Someone shoved a cigarette into my mouth. Still filled with horror at the memory of their fallen comrade, they pulled me from my stupor. "You must be strong, Luba Leontievna. You are going home! Be calm!" they repeated.

When I had recovered I thanked the men. My guard and I set out for our walk back to the camp. As we passed through the small village of Potyma, I suddenly started to run toward the village's tiny post office. "Stop! Stop! Stop or I will have to shoot!" my frantic guard shouted, sprinting after me.

Fortunately, by the time my inexperienced guard had caught up to me I was safely inside the post office. "I'm not trying to escape. I only want to send a telegram to my family," I called through the door. I took a telegram form from a stack on the counter and tried to compose a message to my family, but my hand trembled so violently I could not write.

The proprietress, observing my plight, offered to help. "You dictate the message and I will write it. What do you want to tell them?"

"Tell them . . . tell them I'm free!" I exclaimed.

"I'll tell them that you are free and well," the proprietress said, placing a glass of water in my trembling hands.

Suddenly I remembered that I had no money to pay for the telegram and I began to weep hysterically.

"Hush, poor prisoner," the woman said sadly. "I will send your telegram this minute. You do not have to pay me. It is we who should repay you."

19 FREEDOM

The next day I embarked on my journey home, for which I had waited for seven years. But to my distress, I could not rouse myself to the ecstasy I had always expected to feel. Instead I sat as if I were drugged, gaping out the train window, unable to sustain a coherent thought. I stared at the ramshackle Siberian villages spotted along the railroad tracks like miniature prison camps.

Our train, a regular passenger train, carried others besides prisoners, and I tried to fix my attention on two rosy-cheeked toddlers who played in the aisle. But I could not concentrate on the children. Instead I found myself examining every passenger, unnerved to discover that I could discern instantly which were released prisoners like me. Were my eyes as glazed, my cheeks as sunken as theirs? Was I, too, branded with the mark of a prisoner in a way that would always distinguish me from other people—even my family?

My family had received my telegram and were waiting for me when the train pulled into Moscow's Severnaya Station. The moment I touch them, the deadness inside me will disappear, I told myself.

But at that moment a strange detachment possessed me, and I suddenly felt as if I was the audience, not the actor, in my own greatest drama. I stepped off the train and fell into Zhan's arms. He patted me awkwardly. "Don't worry. It is all over, Lubasha." I turned to the others and felt the embraces of my brother Styopa and my sister Ira. My own children, three young adult strangers whom I scarcely recognized, hung back. Finally they greeted me with the warm word *"Mamochka,"* but their kisses were cold and formal.

"Where are Momma and Dunya?" I cried. Zhan again was embracing me, but would not answer my question. "Auntie Dunya is still alive," I heard my daughter Ira say quietly, and with a stab of sorrow I understood her unspoken message. My mother was dead.

As we drove home through Moscow's familiar streets, Zhan sat beside me in the car, trying to sustain a cheerful conversation. My children in the back seat forced a few polite words when the silence became strained and awkward. All of us were relieved to arrive at our apartment.

I stepped inside my beautiful Bolshoi apartment and as I did, memories of the hundreds of bouquets of flowers which had filled the apartment after the birth of each of my children and after my first performance with Yakhoncov rose to meet me. Now a single bouquet of carnations stood on the dining-room table. Zhan presented them to me and declared, "We are all so happy to see you home again, Lubasha." His words sunk like stones in my heart, and I could not bring myself to fully believe them.

Mechanically I hung my coat in the hallway on the same hook from which I had pulled it seven years ago on my way out the door with the MGB. "Where is Dunya?" I asked when I returned to face my family. My sister Ira pointed to Dunya's bedroom, took my hand, and started to lead me toward the door. "I want to go alone," I said, shrugging her away and walking down the hall as if I were approaching a shrine.

Half lying, half sitting, propped by a pillow, my nanny, my second mother, lay dozing. For the first time on that disappointing day emotion surged through me. I wanted to cry and clutch Dunya, but I restrained myself and instead settled beside her, stroking her hand as she had mine when I was a child. As always, Dunya wore a white kerchief on her head, and slowly her old eyes opened with a dim and distant stare. "It's me! It's me—your Lubasha." I cradled her to me, but Dunya's vacant eyes told me she had not recognized me. I let her frail body fall back on the pillow and I knelt by her bed, shaking it with wrenching sobs swelled by ten years of grief.

Through this storm, I felt someone embracing me and an unfamiliar voice saying, "Lubov Leontievna, please . . . please calm yourself. Here is a drink of water. Please drink it. Let me help you."

I lifted my eyes to the first voice which had spoken tenderly to me that day and met Fenia, a young girl whom Zhan had hired to care for Dunya. It was Fenia who explained that only she, Dunya, and Zhan still lived in my apartment. "Both Lyonya and Ira are married," Fenia said. "Vladik is in college. He lives with Zhan's parents."

When I had composed myself enough to return to my family, I congratulated my two eldest children on their marriages. "But where is your wife, Lyonya? And your husband, Ira?" I asked, a shade of accusation in my voice. Perhaps you are ashamed to introduce me, I thought but did not say.

"They are coming soon, Lubasha," Zhan soothed. "We didn't want to surprise you too greatly at the railroad station." That evening I met Ira's husband Leon, an engineer, and Lyonya's wife Marina, an exquisite, elegant young woman from a cultured Moscow family.

Ironically, it was Marina from whom I felt the first genuine spark of warmth and understanding in my family. She embraced me and began to weep when we were introduced. "Dear Luba Leontievna. Your children and Zhan Fydorovich have told me so much about you that I have already learned to love you and want to be like you. Please consider me your daughter."

Why should Marina love me and my own children be so cold? I thought suspiciously as I observed them during dinner, struggling—it seemed to me—to accept me. At the end of the dinner Lyonya, now twenty-two and a lawyer like Zhan, offered the first toast. He lifted a glass of champagne and said, "For my beautiful, gray *Mamochka*." He came around the table and kissed me on the head, but his kind words could not remove the wall I felt between us.

During the first weeks of my return, Zhan treated me like the ill person I undoubtedly was, trying not to talk about prison or touch any subject that would distress me. But I burned with a fever of disappointment with my family and would not be consoled. Zhan's silence only widened the chasm between us, until I had convinced myself that not only my children but even my husband despised me.

I, completely gray, was certain that I looked at least ten years older than my handsome husband, whose few flecks of gray had only made him seem more distinguished. One day my sister Ira suggested that I should dye my hair and I flew into a rage, certain that her recommendation was yet another sign of my family's rejection.

"I know you have suffered, Lubasha. But you must believe that all of your family suffered with you. Why are you so irritable to us?" Ira tried to calm me.

But her words only chafed my sore feelings. How could my family ever understand the agonies of my ten years apart from them? What was worse, they did not seem to me to sincerely try. Every day of those ten years I had yearned for them, but sometimes I suspected they had scarcely even missed me. They had married and worked and celebrated holidays without me. My return, I sensed, had disrupted their routine. I was an embarrassment to them at worst, an inconvenience at best.

Styopa, now nearly sixty and aged beyond his years, also tried to reason with me. "You're not fair to Zhan, Lubasha," Styopa scolded. "You are not giving him a chance."

"Do any of you think about being fair to me?" I snapped, taking offense at my brother's words. "For ten long years I gave myself to helping others. Now, when I need help, I am shunned."

For hours I sat by Dunya's bed, the only person in the world who might have understood me, but I found no flicker of recognition from my old and dying nanny. Only Marina, my new daughter-in-law, seemed to me to make the effort to appreciate all the suffering my gray hairs represented, and I spent hours with her, relieved to be away from Zhan. Marina took me shopping and escorted me to theatres and concerts. It was with Marina I first stepped back into the Bolshoi, where I did not see even one familiar face.

Besides the excursions with Marina, I spent hours alone at my mother's grave, speaking aloud to her, not caring if passersby thought me mad. Drop by drop I had eked out the story of my mother's death from my family who, again misjudging me, had thought it wisest to spare me sorrow. But I was determined to hear every detail of my mother's last days. Finally Zhan told me that my mother, who had been paralyzed the last ten days of her life, had repeatedly drawn my name with her finger on her bedcover.

The sorest subject between Zhan and me arose one day when I was visiting with Larisa, a friend from Potyma Prison, who had also been recently released and with whom I could converse far more easily than with my family. Larisa's husband, Leonid, had died shortly before Larisa was released from prison. "But my tormentors weren't satisfied to kill him with grief," she said. "You know, of course, that a decree was passed by Stalin which states that any prisoner separated from a spouse for more than three years is automatically divorced. The authorities had told Leonid it was to protect him from being contaminated by my crime!"

I rushed home in a rage and confronted Zhan, who sadly admitted the truth. "Yes, Lubasha, we are officially divorced. I was going to tell you. But we can remarry."

"Why didn't you tell me?" I screamed.

"I want to forget your past as much as you do, Lubasha," Zhan said crossly. "But ten years is a long time. And you cannot blame me for thinking you could not have sat in prison for ten years without a reason. Are you sure you were not at least a little at fault?"

"I will never forgive you for those words," I hissed, my fury so great I could only whisper. "What the government could never do with its decrees, you have accomplished with your suspicion."

"But, Lubasha, I am only asking you to look at the situation from our point of view," Zhan pled. "Do totally innocent people spend ten years in prison?" I fled from the room, my heart filled with hatred.

From that day on my estrangement with Zhan widened, and whenever he tried to raise the subject of our relationship, I silenced him haughtily, blaming him now not only for his own suspicions, but also the coldness of our children. If Zhan doubted me, surely it was no wonder my own children could not bring themselves to completely believe my innocence and show me the tenderness I ached for.

On a cold day in October, already portending winter, I decided to talk to Zhan. Many of the other prisoners I knew were undergoing traumas as terrible as mine with their families. Like cave-dwellers emerging into the light after years of darkness, we had stumbled into freedom; and perhaps it was not entirely our families' fault if we could not swiftly adjust. Perhaps I had become so accustomed to life inside prison that I would never be able totally to adjust again to the world outside.

As calmly as I could, I reproached Zhan for my family's coldness. "You will never know how you have wounded me," I said and began to weep.

"But, Lubasha," Zhan said, "you have become so difficult, and you refuse to try to understand us. The children grew up with you gone, and now they must learn to know you. It was not easy for them to have a mother in prison and their teachers constantly telling them that you were an American spy. It was terribly hard for both me and the children. I remember the day Irachka came home from school crying because her teacher had shamed her. She was sitting with a girl whose parents were Communist Party members. The teacher scolded Ira's friend, 'How dare you sit with that girl whose mother is an enemy of the state!' "

As logically as ever, Zhan presented his case; but by the time he paused, my heart was bursting with hatred. "It's your fault! It's entirely your fault!" I screamed. "You could have countered the lies the children were taught at school! But of course you did not believe in me yourself. Even the government released me because of my innocence. But you still consider me guilty!" I cried.

At this moment a scream burst through the fire of our fight. "It's Fenia . . . she's in Dunya's room," I gasped, dashing down the hall.

"She's dying!" Fenia cried. I clasped Dunya and held her to me for the last five minutes of her life.

With Dunya dead and Zhan as well as dead to me, I decided I must leave my home. One October day when Zhan was at work and I was alone in the apartment, I wrote a cold, curt note to Zhan: "I am leaving. I will never return. Do not try to find me. You and the children should forget me." Calmly, and not permitting myself a moment's memory of the happiness that had surrounded me in my apartment before my imprisonment, I stepped out its doors forever.

At the time of my release, I had received a permit to return to Moscow to live in my apartment. However my passport, unaltered since Marinsk, did not authorize me to live anywhere else in Moscow. When I walked away from my home, I rushed to the Moscow Housing Commission and pled for reassignment to another apartment. In my desperation to find a place to live, I endured the humiliation of explaining my estrangement from my family.

The woman official with whom I spoke had heard hundreds of similar stories before. "People like you are coming in every day. I don't know why prisoners can't get along better with their families," she huffed. "You ought to be grateful to have a roof to come home to. There's no space for you now, Comrade," she said. "It may take months, or even years, but I'll put your name on the waiting list," was all the reassurance the woman would offer.

Thus I left my own apartment not only with nowhere else to live, but with the knowledge that my friends could only legally invite me to stay in their homes for three nights at a time and not more than three visits all together. Fortunately, since Stalin's death and with the demographic upheaval caused by mass rehabilitation of prisoners, enforcement of such laws had become less strict. In any case, I did not fear to violate the unjust rule which tried to prevent me from living in my own city, but I did hesitate to incriminate my friends who could be subject to jail and fined for housing me more than three times.

Nevertheless, it was to my friends whom I had known in prison that I now turned, and from them I sought the sympathy which only other prisoners could provide. The first friend who took me in was Polina, a young woman I had met in Potyma. Polina's parents had both died in the early thirties in Stalin's prisons when Polina was still a child. Already embittered as a teen-ager, Polina had remarked to a friend, "If Stalin had died, my parents would have lived!" Her comment was overheard and reported to the MGB, who sent the young Polina to prison. In Potyma, Polina, with no relatives, had come to regard me as family, and now she pled with me to stay in her apartment. "I don't care if they arrest me, Lubasha," she insisted. "I'm not afraid of them anymore."

For the next three years, living as an exile in my own city, I did stay many months with dear Polina, to whom I felt closer than to my own children. But during those three years I was also cared for by many other former prisoners whom I had known and even by their prisoner friends whom I had not met before. Among us there was a rapport which almost none of us found in our own families. We spent hours swapping prison experiences, a diversion which surprisingly brought considerable consolation to us who could not swiftly shed our Gulag identity.

As the months wore on I no longer felt hatred toward my family, but only a deep disappointment and regret. They and I stood on two sides of a huge canyon, probably impossible to span, and in any event I did not even have the strength to try.

For ten years I had been on a journey of horror, kept alive only by anticipating the end of my sentence and the return home to my family. Slowly I came to understand that through those ten years I had imbued our reunion with impossible expectations, and it was not entirely my family's fault that these had not been fulfilled.

Even during the most terrible times of my imprisonment, the prospect of reunion with my family had always provided at least a thread of hope. Now even that had been severed, and I was as adrift as my hopes. Only the former prisoners in whose society I now spent my time could understand my loss.

In prison I had become known as Luba the ballerina—the proud woman who always holds her head high. Now outside the prison I found myself slinking around Moscow's streets, terrified of an encounter with my family—almost as much a fugitive in my freedom as I had felt in Siberia's prisons.

Without a residence permit I could not work, and with no job to occupy me I first spent days caged in Polina's apartment, fearful that I might meet my family if I stepped outside. Restless and miserable inside, I could not stay indoors forever and started to walk the streets of Moscow. I spent hours staring at shop windows, always watching warily for my family. Often I spent entire days in a cinema, watching the same film over and over. At least once each week I spent almost the entire day at the cemetery where Momma and Dunya were buried.

Although I refused to call Zhan or the children, when winter came I did call my sister Ira to ask her to bring me my winter coat from Zhan's apartment. Ira berated me and wept bitterly. "How can you do this to your own family, Lubasha? Zhan and the children and Styopa and I have been sick from worry with no word of you. How can you be so childish and cruel?"

"They don't care, Ira. They don't need me. They don't even believe I was innocent. It was they who threw me out . . . Life has thrown me out," I said wearily to my sister.

One winter afternoon, with plump flakes of Moscow snow flying in my face, I paused in my wanderings before the Bolshoi Theatre. I lifted my face to the snow, but the gentle fall of flakes did not comfort me. I leaned against one of the tall, thick white pillars on the Bolshoi's portico and wept.

"*Mamochka, Mamochka!*" I cried, longing for the one person in the world who would have understood me and could have advised me. "There is nowhere to turn," I said aloud, walking away from the Bolshoi. That afternoon, with all my sufficiency exhausted, I walked and repeated the words of an Orthodox prayer I had heard from childhood: "Lord Jesus Christ, have mercy on me, a sinner. Lord Jesus Christ, have mercy on me, a sinner." The words washed over me with comfort and also brought back an experience from prison I had nearly buried.

In the middle of one of Marinsk's worst winters, I and a group of women had been at the Marinsk station when a trainload of male political prisoners arrived from Moscow. We watched with pity as the men staggered out of the train, emaciated, freezing, and ill. Suddenly a tall man, so thin he seemed a skeleton, appeared at the door of the railroad car. Hatless, barefooted, and obviously too feeble to walk, he was supported by two other prisoners. Only a light summer shirt and torn trousers covered his scarecrow body. But from the face of this half-dead body shone penetrating blue eyes, filled with kindness and life.

With a cry of pity we women ran toward the poor man, pulling off our jackets to give to him. When I covered him with a jacket, he made the sign of the cross over me. "He's a priest," one of the men at his side said, a fact which somehow made his suffering even more pitiful to me and the other women, and I began to weep.

The priest lifted his head toward us and began to speak and even the guards, moved by the authority of this man, did not try to silence him. "Don't cry over me, sisters," he said. "Remember how Jesus Christ suffered. I am happy to experience this suffering for my faith and for the love of God. Remember how our Lord Jesus Christ suffered for us. Believe in him and it will be easier for you to carry your cross."

That winter day as I walked the streets of Moscow I pondered this episode and also recalled the old woman whom I had met in Marinsk. She had spoken nearly the same words as the priest. The only truly strong people I had ever known in my life, I reflected, were my mother, the priest, and the old woman I had met in Marinsk, who was also a Christian believer. For a moment a spark of hope tantalized me, but then it flickered and died. "Those people were all holy—even saints," I told myself. "It requires holiness to follow God. It would be contemptible for me in my sinful state to even try."

Thus God, I convinced myself, was distant and unknowable, except to the holy. But my friends, thank God, if he did exist, could talk and touch me with their comfort, and I turned to them more desperately than ever, moving from place to place to avoid arrest.

After I left my home, I at first returned frequently to the Housing Commission to request a room and was always met with the same dismal reply: "You have an apartment, comrade. If you refuse to live there, all you can do is wait patiently for another place." In January 1959, more than three years after I had left home, I returned once again after several months to the Housing Commission.

"Bershadskaya, we have been holding a voucher for a room for you for several weeks," the young man at the desk said when I gave him my name, "but since you left no address, we could not send it to you."

My new home was a room of nine square meters located on the third floor of a six-story house on Shchepok Street. The room was small and empty, and I had to share a communal bathroom and kitchen, but it was mine. Now with a residence permit I would find a job teaching ballet. I would have privacy, peace, and independence. I asked my sister for a few pieces of furniture. All my friends brought me flowers and housewarming gifts, and I settled into my room. My journey is over, I told myself. At last I will be happy.

20 CONVERSION

The happiness I had hoped to find in my new apartment in Moscow—like all the prospects of happiness which I had pursued after my release from prison—was fleeting.

Feeling as a fugitive in Moscow where I constantly feared I might encounter my family, I moved to Sochi. I had found healing there after my first release from prison and hoped the sea would again be a balm to restore my strength. But although I spent hours alone staring at the sea, seeking its solace, I could not find the peace I sought.

In 1963 I remarried. Nick Roitburd, a Jewish artist, possessed like me a passion to emigrate from the Soviet Union. In Sochi, a port city, Nick and I studied every foreign ship that docked, dreaming how we might be transported to the forbidden, faraway lands which the ships represented. I was now so desperate to leave the Soviet Union I believed I did not care where I went if only I could leave behind the motherland that had betrayed me and the memories which tortured me.

In our most farfetched schemes, Nick and I could not have envisioned how our dream would come true. In 1967, after the Six Day War in Israel, the Soviet government began to permit a trickle of Jews to emigrate from the U.S.S.R. to Israel. Because Nick was Jewish he was eligible to emigrate and take me with him.

But our escape, at last theoretically legal, was not so simple. Fearful of an exodus if permission was granted to all Jews who wished to emigrate, the Soviet government erected innumerable obstacles, nearly as difficult to surmount as Siberia's prison walls. Desperate and determined to leave, Nick and I haunted OVIR, the office which issued visas to Jewish emigrants.

After three years, in July 1970, our persistence was finally rewarded. Nick and I left Moscow with two hundred dollars, a few photographs of the families we were leaving behind, and the pleas of our friends, "Use your freedom. Tell the world about us!"

In Israel I wavered between ecstasy at my new freedom and despair at my loneliness for Russia. I was tormented with doubts. Had I made the right choice to sever myself forever from my homeland, not only the setting of so much horror in my life, but also of my childhood and early adult happiness?

Soon after our arrival in Israel, I was invited by an American Jewish organization to tour the United States to speak on behalf of the hundreds of thousands of Soviet Jews still wishing to emigrate from the U.S.S.R. In two months I spoke in twenty-seven cities in the United States and Canada, addressing several thousand Americans in meetings and press and television interviews. I welcomed the opportunity to visit the country of the Americans of whom I had so many fond memories from my days of working at the American Embassy during World War II.

After I returned to Israel, I grew increasingly restless. Nick and I found Israel's culture especially foreign to Russia's and the Hebrew language terribly difficult to learn. Neither Nick nor I could find jobs in our own professions when we arrived in Israel, and as the months passed we could scarcely find any jobs at all. Israel, we sadly decided, would not become our home.

Determined to leave Israel, Nick and I worked at every job we could find until we had earned enough money to purchase two tickets to Europe, where, we were convinced, we would find a culture more kindred to our own Russia.

On April 25, 1972, on my fifty-sixth birthday we flew to Brussels, Belgium, a European city chosen at random. In beautiful Brussels we at last believed we had found a home. However, when we went to the police station to register the day after we arrived in Brussels, we discovered we could only settle there if we could provide proof of employment or adequate finances to support ourselves.

Although the Belgian officials were courteous, they could not offer us a solution. "You are welcome to visit our country for three months," they told us. "After that you will be deported to Israel."

Once again our hopes, which had been raised so high, were hurled to the ground.

After a month, unable to speak the language or find employment in Brussels, the little money we had brought from Israel was rapidly disappearing. Near the end of all our resources, we found ourselves in a pit of despair with no strength to pull ourselves from it and no one to help lift us. One last possibility hung in the back of both of our minds, but neither of us could bring ourselves to mention it. It was Nick who finally said one day, "We don't have any choice, Lubasha. We will have to return to Russia."

That same day, we forced ourselves to obtain directions to the Soviet Consulate from our hotel clerk. That night we lay awake in agony at the move we planned to make the next day, certain we had no place else to turn.

After the massacre at Kengir, I was certain that some part of me had died. Now with every step toward the embassy, I felt the life that remained draining from me. Even in prison my pride had not permitted me to bow before my oppressors. Now I had become a cringing creature, a slave crawling before the masters I hated.

Inside the building marked in large black letters, Soviet Consulate, Nick and I were summoned to a reception desk. It was Nick who found the words to state our request. I stood beside him, feeling no more will than a leaf in the wind.

In the same listless state, I followed Nick to the office of a consulate official, a handsome young man who greeted us cordially in Russian and introduced himself. "And please tell me your names," he beamed. I sat silently while Nick introduced us both. As soon as Nick mentioned my name, the mask of politeness on the official's face vanished. "Luba Bershadskaya!" he bellowed. "You are the Luba Bershadskaya who toured all over the United States slandering the Soviet Union. And you dare ask to return to the motherland? You will never see my country again!"

A surge of rage suddenly suffused my lifeless body. "It is my country as well as yours. I have as much right to live there as you do!" I shouted.

"Get out, and if you ever come back I will call the police to carry you away!" the officer yelled back, pointing Nick and me to the door.

In the past—through all my sufferings in Siberia and through all the miseries in Moscow after my release from prison—I had always pushed all thoughts of dying from me. Death, like a boulder, had hovered above me and had often come close to crushing me. Now I no longer had strength to resist and I felt my own death to be imminent. The boulder which I had held away so long would finally fall and grind me to the ground.

"Momma, if you see me from heaven, tell me what to do," I wept and prayed, not knowing where else to turn. Even without my mother to guide me, I believed I knew her reply. "Yes, you made a terrible mistake, Lubasha, when you severed yourself from your family and your country and tried to enter into another world where you are unwanted."

With nothing else to occupy our time, Nick and I spent hours wandering the streets of Brussels, trying to stave off thoughts of the future.

One Thursday morning as we walked past blocks of cozy, comfortable Belgian apartments, I, who had always been so aware of appearances, could not stop weeping. I thought of the cheap hotel where we were living and moaned to Nick, "We won't even be able to stay there much longer. Where will we go?"

"It will not help to cry about it in public," Nick reminded me gently and tried to steer me down a side street where I would be seen by fewer people. "Let's turn here," he said.

Without knowing why, I pulled away from Nick and hurried ahead to the next block. "I want to turn down this street, not that one," I called back to Nick.

As certainly as I had known that I should turn at that specific street, I also felt drawn down it, as surely as if someone were leading me by the hand. I hurried down my street, startling Nick who trailed behind.

Suddenly, I thought I heard Russian singing. Afraid to trust my own perceptions, I summoned Nick. "Hurry, come . . . the singing . . . it's Russian . . . can you hear it?" I panted.

We rushed toward the singing and as we did the words of a Russian Orthodox chant met us, "Gospodi, Pomiluy . . . Lord, have mercy."

But still we could not find the source of the wonderful sound. I saw no sign of a church, only houses. But I would not stop searching. I held my ear against one door, then another, until the music was clear and strong.

When I opened the door to the house, singing surrounded me. I stepped inside and, although I had not worshiped in an Orthodox church since I accompanied my mother to St. Sofia's as a child in Kiev, the church felt familiar. As I worshiped now, I felt myself strangely—almost palpably—lifted.

Through the worst terrors of prison—including the massacre at Kengir—I had sometimes had the sensation of being upheld by hands which I could not identify. I had attributed the feeling to my imagination or simply my own strength. However, the tragedies of my life since leaving prison had convinced me that my own strength could not be the source. Somehow, I knew I must search elsewhere for the serenity I so desperately desired.

That day at Trinity Church, a small Russian Orthodox Church in Brussels, marked my return to the pursuit of God, a pursuit which I now realized had begun at my mother's side. I, however, had permitted both the joys and sorrows of my eventful life to divert me from that path. Like a willful child, I had pulled myself away from the God to whom my mother had introduced me and I had stumbled alone, stubborn and headstrong, through all of my life.

More starving than I had ever felt in Siberia for food, I now nearly lived at Trinity Church, seeking for God. Nick and I waited eagerly for Saturdays and Sundays when services were held, and we were the first to arrive at the church and the last to leave.

During these weeks, I began to pray—timidly at first, weighed by the certainty of my unworthiness and sin. Slowly I began to speak to God—simply, openly, and more confidently. One Saturday evening as I stood praying before a painting of Christ, I suddenly felt God's presence, peace, and power cloaking me and I did not want to leave the church.

I rushed to the church the next morning but could not concentrate on the Sunday service. I sat staring at the painting of Christ and longed for the sense of His presence that I had experienced so powerfully the night before. "God, why can't I feel you? Why can't I see you?" I prayed. But I felt so empty and lonely I had trouble focusing my thoughts on Him. I began to wonder if my experience last night had really happened.

Then, suddenly, I heard a voice speaking, "Look, the Father is before you." I turned and a figure suffused with light appeared in front of me. He was plainly visible, but His face was veiled. A deep contentment spread over me, even as I wondered why I couldn't see His face. All that day I basked in the afterglow of the vision, with only a tiny corner of my mind puzzling over why His face was hidden from me.

That evening Nick and I sat in our hotel room reading. Nick, who was reading the Bible, suddenly said, "Do you know, Lubasha, that when Moses wanted to see God he was not allowed to see His face?"

I leaped from my chair like a crazy person and cried, "Why did you say that? What caused you to raise that particular subject?"

"I don't know, Lubasha," Nick said, bewildered by my excitement. "The thought simply came to my mind as I read."

During the first weeks after Nick and I began attending Trinity Church I sought God frantically, like a child, darting in every direction, searching for any clue that might bring me closer to Christ. One day as I was praying, I understood that God had been waiting and beckoning to me all my life. With a slow and steady pace, I walked toward the hands which had been always held out to me.

Even after I had been released from prison in 1956, I had not been able to shed my Gulag identity. Eerily, I sometimes felt as if I were still wearing my black prison uniform and would often touch my garments to reassure myself that the hideous remnant of prison was truly gone.

My conversion to Christ not only transformed my life, but also brought a flood of forgiveness and peace from God to me. One day as I was reading the New Testament and contemplating Christ's words, I had the sensation that my black prison uniform and all the sin it symbolized was removed. In its place I felt myself clothed in a white silken dress of divine forgiveness.

It was also my encounter with Christ which enabled me to bear the sufferings of my life and even see divine significance in them. When I met Christ I at last understood the words of two unforgettable Christians I had met in Siberia during my imprisonment. "Christ will walk with you through your sufferings and lead you to his kingdom," the *babushka* in Marinsk had promised. "Believe in Christ and it will be easier to carry your cross," a priest whom I had also met in Marinsk had encouraged us prisoners.

Through my ten terrible years in the Gulag I had been cast down. But I had not been forsaken. I had seen spirits soiled and bodies brutalized. In Kengir my friends had been mangled before my eyes. Through this torment, I now knew I had been preserved by God's strong hands.

Before I entered prison when I was thirty years old and at the pinnacle of my promising career and secure in my happy family, I believed I had lived life to the full. Without my sufferings, I now know my life would not have been fully formed. Had it not been for my sufferings, I believe I would not have found God.

Since my conversion in Brussels, I have walked with Christ who lifted my trampled life from the ground. He has led me in paths which have wound through both light and darkness.

Through the kindness of Russian friends Nick and I met at Trinity Church and at the Tolstoy Foundation in Brussels, we were able to emigrate to the United States in 1973. In the United States we were generously resettled by the headquarters of the Tolstoy Foundation in New Jersey. We lived in New Jersey only four years before my husband, Nick, died from cancer in 1977.

Through all the events of my life since 1972, Christ has been beside me. I know His touch.